THE
FOG

About the Authors

Rob MacGregor has written several books on New Age topics and has won the Edgar Allan Poe award in mystery writing.

Bruce Gernon is a pilot who has flown extensively in the Caribbean. He has appeared in many documentaries about the Bermuda Triangle. Both Gernon and MacGregor live in South Florida, on the edge of the Bermuda Triangle.

THE FOG

A Never Before Published Theory of the Bermuda Triangle Phenomenon

Rob MacGregor and Bruce Gernon

Llewellyn Publications
Woodbury, Minnesota

First Edition
First Printing, 2005

Book design and layout by Joanna Willis
Cover cloud imagery © 2004 Digital Vision
Cover design by Lisa Novak
Cover plane image © 2005 by Bruce Gernon
Illustration of Bimini island courtesy of J. Manson Valentine; recreated
    by Llewellyn art department
Interior images courtesy of authors except for maps on pages xix and
    131 by Llewellyn art department

Llewellyn is a registered trademark of Llewellyn Worldwide, Ltd.

Library of Congress Cataloging-in-Publication Data
MacGregor, Rob.
    The fog : a never before published theory of the Bermuda Triangle
    phenomenon / Rob MacGregor and Bruce Gernon.
        p. cm.
    Includes bibliographical references and index.
    ISBN 0-7387-0757-0
        1. Bermuda Triangle. I. Gernon, Bruce. II. Title.

G558.M33 2005
001.94—dc22   2005044334

Llewellyn Publications
A Division of Llewellyn Worldwide, Ltd.
2143 Wooddale Drive, Dept. 0-7387-0757-0
Woodbury, MN 55125-2989, U.S.A.
www.llewellyn.com

Printed in the United States of America

In memory of
Bruce Gernon, Sr.
&
Donald R. MacGregor,
the authors' fathers

Contents

PART 2: Beyond the Fog

PART 3: Seeing the Fog

Figures

Foreword

In the last fifteen years of investigating the notorious and much-maligned Bermuda Triangle, I've come across many witnesses to unusual events. They've all had one thing in common: they were seeking an explanation for what happened to them. Many times I felt frustrated when trying to record their accounts. I was asking them for information, but invariably that is what they were seeking from me—an answer, often an easy and quick one.

That's not an easy thing to give. It's difficult to say what could have happened to those who encountered unusual incidents involving electromagnetic aberrations, compasses spinning wildly, navigational equipment going on the fritz, the horizon vanishing, strange vapors and fogs forming around them, or unusual glowing lights encompassing them. All that I definitely could say was that it did happen and that they were among the "lucky ones."

Strange events are inexorably associated with that area of the Caribbean. More airplanes and ships have disappeared in the Bermuda Triangle than in any other place in the world. Are these phenomena connected? Even after collating the data of dozens upon dozens of stories of people who experienced the phenomena, it remained difficult to say what specifically caused these incidents.

Then Bruce Gernon introduced himself to me. He knew of my research from a website I started in 1999. He was different from all the others. From reading the old books on the subject, I recognized the name immediately. I was indeed surprised to hear from him. I didn't know that anyone else had been thoroughly investigating the Bermuda Triangle over the last decade.

Bruce was different from the others who'd told me their stories. He was not content to casually puzzle over his experience, explain it away, or try to forget it. He was the only one who personally set out to crack the mystery. By the year 2000 his investigation had spanned roughly thirty years. He is an excellent in situ observer who has traveled the Triangle extensively and is always willing to frankly discuss what happened to him and how his experience might relate to other disappearances.

The publication of *The Fog* will be the first time that any witness and survivor of phenomena related to the Bermuda Triangle has ever written a book, not only detailing his experience, but also presenting a new theory about the mystery.

While Bruce is witness and researcher, Rob MacGregor is a serious investigator of mysterious phenomena and the author of many books. Both men have lived on the edge of the Bermuda Triangle and flown into it many times. In the years that I've known Bruce and Rob, they have always kept me informed of recent developments. So, when a young scientist named Ivan Lima contacted me and told me of his experience, I referred the information to Bruce. It was not long before Bruce and Rob were airborne and flying to meet with Dr. Lima in Fort Lauderdale at a restaurant located at the site of the former naval base where Flight 19 departed and set off the mystery of the Triangle.

As my research continues into the Bermuda Triangle, I am sure that I will encounter Bruce again. When aboard a ship, I can imagine that I'll hear the drone of his aircraft above and see the dip of his wings in recognition. Whenever I was called upon to recommend people to film for television documentaries, I was always ready and happy to mention Bruce Gernon. But here he is finally able to tell his story his way.

Bruce indeed holds the key to a fascinating mystery, and this book will help readers unlock the enigma of the Bermuda Triangle. Bruce approaches the subject seriously, with no motivation other than trying to uncover its secrets for the benefit of others. He is not just interested in merely recording events, but finding answers and preventing the Triangle from claiming more victims.

Gian J. Quasar
Author of *Into the Bermuda Triangle*
Webmaster of Bermuda-triangle.org
March 13, 2005

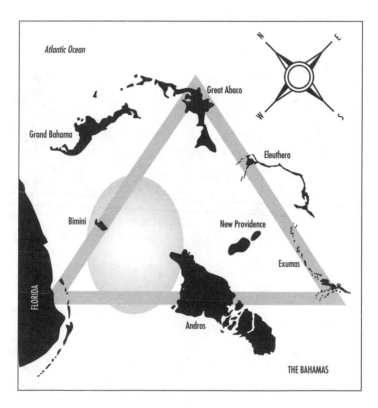

Figure 1—The Bermuda Triangle

Introduction

What Is Electronic Fog?

> *Bruce Gernon offers a plausible solution to the disap-*
> *pearance of Flight 19. There have been many docu-*
> *mented cases of knowledgeable and experienced pilots*
> *encountering electromagnetic disturbances.*
>
> —WALTER HOUGHTON
> Assistant director, Broward County, Florida,
> Aviation Department, and professor of aviation,
> Broward Community College

"Nothing on my map of Florida corresponded with the earth's features I had seen. . . .Where could I be?"

Those were the baffling words of Charles Lindbergh as he described a mysterious experience on a flight across the Caribbean, through the heart of the Bermuda Triangle.

Lindbergh took off at 1:35 AM on February 13, 1928, on what, for him, should have been a routine flight, the last leg of his around-the-Gulf and Caribbean tour. He intended to fly nonstop from Havana to St. Louis, which would be the first-ever nonstop flight between the two cities. "It should have been an easy flight—about a third the distance from New York to Paris," he wrote in his autobiography.

He climbed to an altitude of 4,000 feet and settled back to enjoy the night flight. "But halfway across the Straits of Florida my magnetic compass started rotating, and the earth-inductor-compass needle jumped back and forth erratically. By that time a haze had formed, screening off horizons."

Only one other time had he seen two compasses fail at once. That was during a storm in the Atlantic en route to Paris, and his magnetic compass only oscillated back and forth, so he was able to calculate his direction by the central point of the oscillation. But this time, in the Caribbean, the magnetic compass spun in circles and the inductor compass was useless. "I had no idea whether I was flying north, south, east, or west."

Lindbergh started climbing toward the clear sky that just minutes ago had been above him. If he could find Polaris, he could navigate by the stars. But the haze thickened as he climbed higher. So he descended to less than a thousand feet, but the haze followed him and he could barely see the ocean.

Just before dawn, he spotted a shadowy island and assumed that he'd reached the Florida Keys. But after crossing a narrow body of water, Lindbergh saw a long coastline bending to the right, the opposite way that the land curved on his map of Florida. "But if I was not flying over a Florida key, where could I be? Was it possible I had returned to Cuba, that my attempt to read the twirling compasses had put me one-hundred-eighty degrees off course?"

The coastline ended and he saw more keys ahead. He realized that if he wasn't over the Florida Keys, he was above the Bahamas. That meant he'd been flying at a ninety-degree angle from his proper heading and that he was about three hundred miles off course. Once the sun was high enough above the horizon, he determined east and headed through the haze in the opposite direction, toward the Florida coast. The magnetic compass stopped rotating as soon as he reached the mainland. He passed by dozens of heavy squalls as he moved through Florida and Georgia, and headed on to St. Louis to complete his flight.

Possibly because of his renown as a pilot, Lindbergh never talked publicly about his strange experience in what was to become known as the "Bermuda Triangle." He waited to reveal it in his autobiography, which was published four years after his death in 1978. But no doubt he survived the experience, while many others have died, because of his incredible abilities as a pilot.

Lindbergh's experience would be merely an interesting footnote to his flying career and amazing life, and nothing more, were it not for the fact that he documented a case of an aeronautical encounter with a rare but often deadly meteorological phenomenon that remains a scientific anomaly.

Forty-two years later, a pilot named Bruce Gernon encountered a similar fog on a flight from Andros Island in the Caribbean to South Florida. In some respects, Gernon's flight was even more harrowing than Lindbergh's. Gernon not only lost the use of his electronic instruments, but he also experienced a time distortion that puzzled him for years.

Eventually, Gernon came to believe that he had encountered an unclassified geo-meteorological condition that he calls "electronic fog." This fog, he believes, is created by electromagnetic energy released from the earth through water and into the atmosphere. He's also convinced that electronic fog is responsible for many of the strange disappearances of aircraft and boats in the infamous Bermuda Triangle.

Although he once believed that this condition was somehow unique to the Bermuda Triangle, he now believes it can happen elsewhere. In this book, we'll focus on the Caribbean, where Gernon and others flew into electronic fog, and we'll relate it to the Bermuda Triangle legacy.

Several years after his experience, Gernon related his story to Dr. Manson Valentine, then director of the Miami Museum of Science and a leading researcher into the Bermuda Triangle mystery. Dr. Valentine listened closely and asked a number of questions. They met again several months later at a small gathering that included Charles Berlitz, who had already written his most famous book, *The Bermuda Triangle*. At the end of the evening Valentine surprised Gernon with his parting comment, "You must always remember that you hold the key to the Bermuda Triangle."

"It seemed very significant to him that I should understand this," Gernon recalled. "But I was a kid in my twenties, and I just couldn't imagine that I held the key to something so utterly awesome and mysterious."

Years later, however, he would encounter the fog for a second time, and he would recognize something about it that he hadn't previously understood. He discovered why the baffling fog appeared to spread out for miles even though it didn't show up on radar. That was when he knew that he had unraveled an important element related to the mystery of the Bermuda Triangle and that he did indeed hold the key.

Electronic fog is real, dangerous, and mysterious. Unlike any other weather phenomenon, it is linked to distortions in time, and one day could be the key to time travel. The fog is a natural phenomenon, but it also has been reproduced in laboratory experiments, with startling results.

For the most part, science has ignored electronic fog, relegating it to the realm of superstition or misidentification. Scientists are especially leery when they are told of the fog's connection with UFOs, levitation, time travel . . . and the Bermuda Triangle.

It's true that many crashes of airplanes and disappearances of ships in the Caribbean can be explained by regular weather phenomena. But there is more out there than we fully understand. It's the hope of the authors that this book helps clear the air about the fog, and opens the way for new studies of an unusual and significant phenomenon that eventually could change the way we think about life and the way we live it.

PART 1

Into
the
Fog

The Legacy
and the Fog

The sailors, old and young, were gathered at the shell of the abandoned Naval Air Station in Fort Lauderdale. They'd arrived, as they do every year, for a ceremony that has become a ritual, that will go on until all the old sailors who still remember have died. Then it might still go on. The ceremony isn't a commemoration of a battle or a victory, but of a loss, an unexplained loss of five Navy Avenger TBM torpedo bombers that disappeared mysteriously into oblivion on December 5, 1945. The routine training flight turned into a tragedy and sparked a legend when the experienced pilots became disoriented over the Caribbean and never returned. Years later, Flight 19 would be known as the Lost Patrol—even though it wasn't a patrol—and it would mark the cornerstone of the Bermuda Triangle mystery.

A high-school band played a marching song, the Stars and Stripes fluttered in the breeze, and a general was about to address the gathering. At the edge of the crowd, Bruce Gernon, a civilian pilot, watched the proceedings with a special interest.

Gernon felt a strong connection with the pilots of Flight 19. Like them, he encountered mysterious, disorienting conditions over the Caribbean and barely escaped the clutches of a baffling force, an "electronic fog." He believes Flight 19 flew into the same conditions. Like the elusive Loch Ness monster, the force haunting the Bermuda Triangle apparently appears and disappears leaving no trace of its existence in its wake, other than the puzzle of lost vessels and crafts and the stories of those, like Gernon, who survived.

But if Gernon or anyone else in the crowd was hoping that Brigadier General Jerry McAbee would address the lingering question of what happened to the airmen and their planes, he would be disappointed. McAbee wasn't here to talk of the mysteries of the Bermuda Triangle, of strange clouds and odd banks of fog, hovering UFOs, time travel, or electromagnetic anomalies that send compasses into wild spins. Rather, he was here to honor the lost pilots, to carry on the tradition. Even so, there was something surreal about the marching band and the general honoring the flight that set off the Bermuda Triangle saga and the airmen who were last seen stepping from the gigantic spacecraft at the end of Stephen Spielberg's *Close Encounters of the Third Kind*. It almost seemed as if the ceremony were a scene from a movie in the making, and somewhere nearby a director, his storyboard in hand, would yell, "Cut!" And then they'd do it all over again.

When the ceremony was over, Gernon wandered out from the hangar and across the tarmac to the lone Avenger torpedo bomber that had flown in from Jacksonville for the ceremony. It was one of the few remaining in existence and soon attracted a crowd.

A few Navy veterans, who were here in 1945, stood by one wing discussing the disappearance of Flight 19. They seemed to possess an uncanny recollection of every detail, as if it occurred yesterday. Nearby, a crew from *The Learning Channel*, who had arrived from England to film the event as part of a documentary film on the Bermuda Triangle, turned their camera toward the bulky-looking craft. Gian Quasar, the creator of a lively Bermuda Triangle website, took a photo of Gernon by the plane and later added it to his site.

Most of the stories about the Bermuda Triangle are about the loss of lives, and aircraft that vanished without a trace. Gernon, though, is a human survivor of the Bermuda Triangle and has appeared in many of the documentaries about the mystery that have been produced in recent years. Where others have disappeared, Gernon returned with a story of a close encounter with mysterious forces.

At the time of this encounter, he'd never heard of the Bermuda Triangle, but he knew that something significant had happened to him. He thought about it every day and went over every detail. He wanted to make sure that he would remember it just as it happened. Then, more than a year later, he saw an interview on television with two men who were talking about strange events in the Caribbean. They used the term "Bermuda Triangle."

"Suddenly, I realized what happened to me wasn't an isolated event. It was part of something much bigger, and I'd survived it. I'd experienced the Bermuda Triangle first-hand."

A Strange Cloud

Hardly a day goes by when Bruce Gernon doesn't reflect in one way or another on what happened to him one afternoon on a flight more than thirty years ago. He might recall some aspect of the experience, or mention something about it to a friend or acquaintance. Or he might reflect on the entire scenario, which long ago he vowed never to forget.

On the hour drive from the Flight 19 ceremony in Fort Lauderdale to his home in Wellington, Florida, in Palm Beach County, Gernon described his experience in detail. "My dad was a developer and I was a builder, and in 1970 we were searching the Bahamas for an island to build a resort," Gernon began. "We decided on Andros Island, and had made a dozen flights, when on December 4 we encountered something we would never forget."

Gernon was piloting their new Bonanza A36, a stable and smooth-flying aircraft. Even today, more than three decades later, the Bonanza airframe remains relatively unchanged and is one of general aviation's finest performing airplanes. If he had been flying a slower and less stable aircraft that day, Gernon believes that he may not have survived the flight. Although he had planned to take off in the morning, ever the cautious pilot, Gernon delayed the flight until the weather improved. "We waited all morning while it rained and it was close to 3:00 PM when my dad and I, along with Chuck Layfayette, a business associate, took off from Andros Town Airport."

He remembered that the sky was overcast and a light mist was falling. "Weather information wasn't available, so I decided to get airborne, then call Miami Flight Service for atmospheric conditions." As they made a turn after departing the runway, Gernon looked over to the terminal where he saw his friend, John Woolbright, waving to him. Woolbright was a mathematician at the Atlantic Undersea Test Evaluation Center (AUTEC), a navy facility based on the island, which, ironically, would play a role in the Bermuda Triangle mystery.

They climbed to 1,000 feet and assumed a heading of 315 degrees. They couldn't go any higher because of a cloud ceiling at 1,500 feet. "My father was also a pilot and an expert navigator, so we flew the plane together on a direct route to Bimini. We tuned into the Bimini radio beacon on our automatic direction finder, and also used a magnetic compass."

They were cruising at 180 miles an hour and had been flying for about ten minutes when the drizzle ended and the skies cleared. By then, they had reached the northwest end of Andros Island and were flying over the ocean shallows of the Great Bahama Bank. The visibility had improved from about three miles to ten miles and the weather ahead appeared nonthreatening.

As they started to gain altitude, Gernon noticed an almond-shaped lenticular cloud directly in front of them, about a mile away. While other clouds move across the sky with the air currents, lenticular clouds tend to remain stationary. The cloud appeared to be about a mile-and-a-half long and a thousand feet thick, with the top of it reaching an altitude of 1,500 feet. It was white, with smooth edges and appeared inoffensive. However, he found one thing odd about the cloud.

"I'd seen quite a few lenticular-shaped clouds, but never at such a low altitude. They are usually up at 20,000 feet."

But Gernon couldn't spend much time looking at the cloud because he was busy filing his flight plan with the Miami Flight Service. They would fly to Bimini, then directly to West Palm Beach. Miami Radio, the call sign for the flight service, offered a promising forecast. The weather would be clear between Andros and the Florida coast, with a few scattered, isolated thunderstorms of moderate intensity in South Florida. Winds were light and variable, and the temperature was 75 degrees.

By this time, at about ten miles offshore and climbing toward their intended altitude of 10,500 feet, Gernon noticed that the lenticular cloud had changed into a huge, billowy, white, cumulus-shaped cloud. "We were climbing at a thousand feet per minute, and the cloud seemed to be building up underneath us at the same rate that we were ascending."

It rose so quickly that it occurred to him that they were flying over a cumulonimbus cloud, one of the most dangerous to fly through, and that it was about to form a monstrous thunderhead. "Chuck started to get nervous. He had never come this close to a cloud while flying in a small airplane. I assured him that we would break free of it at any moment, and leave it behind."

But after ascending for several minutes, they were nearly one mile high and the cloud was still ascending with them. Then, unexpectedly, the cloud caught up and engulfed the Bonanza. They felt a slight updraft, and visibility was reduced to less than a hundred feet. After about thirty seconds, they broke free of the clouds and continued their ascent.

"But the cloud was still right below us, rising at the same rate," Gernon recalled. "I couldn't even get ten yards above the cloud, and after another half-minute, it closed around us again."

Suddenly, another updraft provided an unexpected burst of acceleration, that pushed them up above the cloud. But then their vertical speed diminished and the cloud caught up to them again. The scenario was repeated at least five more times. "Dad and Chuck were getting worried," Gernon remembered. And Dad suggested we go back to Andros."

Making a 180-degree turn would be risky, but Gernon was considering it when suddenly the airplane broke free again at 11,500 feet and the sky was clear. He leveled the Bonanza and accelerated to a cruising speed of 195 miles per hour.

"What I didn't realize at the time was that the cloud must have been moving horizontally at least 105 miles an hour, our climbing speed, as well as vertically. But when it stopped its horizontal movement, we were finally free of it. When I looked back at the cloud, I was astonished at what I saw. The cloud was still rapidly building, and was enormous. That small lenticular cloud that we had initially flown over had taken on the shape of an immense squall."

But unlike most squalls, which form in a line, this cloud curved in a perfect semicircle and radiated out on either side of them. It appeared to extend out at least ten miles in either direction. After a few minutes, they left the cloud behind and continued on their path toward Bimini under clear skies. "Everything was back to normal, so I engaged the autopilot, sat back, and started to relax."

Trapped

But, after a few minutes, they noticed another squall forming in front of them. "As we approached the cloud, moving at about three miles a minute, an eerie sight began to unfold. To my consternation, the cloud looked very much like the one we'd left behind. It had a similar curving, semicircular shape, except now the arms extended in the opposite direction, directly toward us. The top of this enormous cloud reached at least 40,000 feet."

Then Gernon noticed something else that surprised him. Normal cumulus clouds have a base, or ceiling, one or two thousand feet above the surface. If the cloud is producing rain, the base is usually at about 1,000 feet and sometimes as low as four or five hundred feet. But, as they flew within a few miles of the cloud, he saw that this cloud appeared to emanate directly from the ocean.

"I realized that we couldn't go either under the cloud or above it, and attempting to circumvent it would take us considerably off our flight path. Besides, the arms of the cloud were already stretching out on either side of us, so we couldn't make an easy escape. However, the cloud didn't look too threatening, so after conferring with Dad, I decided to fly into it. I had flown under clouds in heavy rain and I'd penetrated them while flying with instrument-rated pilots, but pilots are supposed to steer clear of strong thunderstorms, and the 10,000-foot level was supposed to be the most dangerous altitude to fly through a storm. I'd been told that there could be updrafts and downdrafts in excess of 100 miles an hour in the heart of a thunderstorm cell."

They were about forty-five miles east of Bimini when they entered the misty edges of this enormous cloud formation. Once inside, Gernon realized he might've made a mistake. Although the cloud was white and fluffy on the outside, its interior was dark, as if night suddenly had fallen.

"But it didn't stay dark for long. Bright white flashes lit up the interior of the cloud. They seemed to go on and off in a neverending, random pattern, and the deeper we penetrated, the more intense the flashes became."

Although there were no bolts of lightning, Gernon had no doubt that they'd entered an electrical storm and were in danger. "When my father asked if I was going to continue on, I didn't have to think very long to answer. I shook my head, turned 135 degrees and assumed a due south heading."

All three men were wearing watches, and they noted that they were deviating from their course at 3:27 PM. An electric-powered clock on the panel, which included a timer that Gernon had engaged upon takeoff, indicated that they'd been airborne for twenty-seven minutes. His father started the timer on his watch when they changed their course, and using very-high frequency OmniRange navigation equipment (VOR), he calculated that they were forty miles southeast of Bimini. Meanwhile, Gernon contacted Miami Radio on the VHF and told them that they had altered their course to avoid a thunderstorm, and they were attempting to fly around it.

"We thought we might be able to avoid the semicircular-shaped cloud to the south, but after traveling six or seven miles, we could see that the cloud continued on our left toward the east. Then, a couple minutes later, we realized that the cloud that we encountered near Andros and the second cloud were now connected. As far as I could tell, the enormous cloud encircled us. I estimated that the diameter of the opening was about thirty miles. We were trapped inside a billowing prison with no way out. We couldn't go over or under it."

The Tunnel Vortex

Gernon's concern was increasing by the minute, but he knew he had to remain calm. He tried to understand how they'd gotten into this predicament. It seemed that the storm was created first in the form of a lenticular cloud just offshore of Andros Island, and then had rapidly spread outward, forming the shape of a donut. He remembered what it was like inside the thunderstorm, and the last thing he wanted to do was fly back into the powerful storm cell.

They'd flown about ten miles from the point where they'd turned south when he noticed a breach in the massive cloud on the west side. The U-shaped aperture, Gernon thought, was where the two arms of the expansive cloud had not yet met.

At the top, on either side, the cloud extended outward in the shape of an anvil. So it looked as if the cloud soon would form a bridge. The anvil shape is commonly seen in cumulonimbus thunderstorms as they reach maturity. The top typically spreads outward for several miles at an elevation of about 35,000 feet. Normally, Gernon would stay clear of such an anvil head, but this time the situation called for drastic action.

"Faced with the dilemma that we were in, I felt that I had no choice but to turn the aircraft 90 degrees to the right and try to exit through the cloud by way of the only visible opening. As we flew toward the aperture, we saw the two anvil heads connect with each other, forming a hole in the cloud. The tunnel was about a mile wide and appeared to be between ten and fifteen miles long. Its bottom was at the 10,000-foot level. On the far side of the passage, we could see blue sky, and that gave us hope."

But as they neared the tunnel, they realized that its diameter was shrinking. Gernon took the engine up to maximum power. By the time they were three miles from the shaft, the opening was only about a thousand feet wide. They were still two miles away when the aperture had shrunk to five hundred feet, and as they entered it, the opening was merely three hundred feet across.

"I recalled what Charles Galanza, my first flight instructor, told us one night during a class. He said that sometimes in the higher altitudes, usually above five-thousand feet, long horizontal tunnels sometimes formed in storm clouds. He called them 'sucker holes,' and warned us never to fly through them. He said he knew of pilots who had tried the feat and were never seen again. I assumed he meant that they'd crashed into the ocean and disappeared."

But by the time the flight was over, Gernon wondered if there were other possibilities.

Weightless

Gernon was startled to see that upon entering the tunnel, strange spiraling lines instantly appeared the entire length of the tunnel. Moments before the tunnel had appeared ten miles long; now it was only about a mile long and he still could see blue sky on the other side. Instead of close to three minutes, it would take only about twenty seconds to get through the tunnel. "I had to remain right in the center of the tunnel, because I was afraid that if the wings ran into the edges of the cloud, I might lose sight of the hole and the path to the clear sky."

The silky white walls of the tunnel glowed with the light from the afternoon sun. The walls appeared to be symmetrical and were slowly shrinking. Along their edges were small puffs of gray clouds about three-feet long and one-foot thick. Gernon noticed that these clouds were swirling around the airplane in a counterclockwise motion at a rate of several times a minute. At the same time, the tunnel continued to shrink around them.

"The diameter was only thirty feet, and the tips of the wings scraped the edges of the cloud as we reached the far side of the tunnel. It had taken about twenty seconds to travel through it. I noticed that contrails formed at the ends of the wings, leaving a parallel trail behind us as we escaped."

That was when he suddenly felt as though he was experiencing zero gravity, and that his seatbelt was the only thing keeping him from levitating out of his seat. "While the vapor trails were streaming from the wings, I felt a strange sensation of weightlessness, and simultaneously a feeling that our speed was increasing."

About ten seconds later, the weightless sensation vanished. "I looked back and gasped as I watched the tunnel walls collapse and form a slowly rotating slit. I was relieved to have made it through the tunnel, but for some reason I felt disoriented, so I asked my dad to check our position. He was always good at using the instruments to give me our exact location on the chart, within a few seconds.

"This time he fiddled with the instruments for longer than usual. Then he told me that something was wrong. That was when I realized that all the electronic and magnetic navigational instruments were malfunctioning. Even the magnetic compass was slowly rotating counterclockwise, as if the plane were making a turn."

Gernon contacted Miami air-traffic control and reported that he wasn't sure of his position and would like radar identification. The plane was equipped with a transponder, a new invention at the time that helped radar controllers identify airplane location. "I told them that we were about forty-five miles southeast of Bimini heading east, and flying at 10,500 feet. But the controller came back and said that there were no planes on radar between Miami, Bimini, and Andros. That was when Dad snatched the microphone and yelled at the controller. 'What the hell do you mean you can't find us on radar?'

"The controller sounded bewildered and apologized, but said the radar showed no blips in the area we were flying. I wondered how this could be. In the past they had always been able to identify us, especially when we were approaching ADIZ, the international defense zone," Gernon recalled.

"Dad was getting more and more agitated and began screaming at the controller. He was starting to panic so I took the microphone back and told the controller to let us know if anything came up on his radar. I did my best to calm Dad and Chuck by saying that we were through the worst of it. Everything would be okay now."

But he was wrong.

"It was about that time that I realized that something very bizarre had happened. Instead of the clear blue sky that we expected at the end of the tunnel, everything appeared a dull grayish white. Visibility appeared to be more than two miles, but there was absolutely nothing to see—no ocean, no horizon, no sky, only a gray haze."

While haze in the lower atmosphere is common, Gernon described it as darker than the common haze that he often encountered. But the air was stable and there was no lightning or precipitation. "We seemed to be in some sort of fog, but unlike the usual fog where visibility is never much over a few hundred feet, we could see much farther." But even more disturbing was the fact that the instruments were still malfunctioning.

An Internal Compass

Gernon slowed the plane down to one hundred and eighty miles an hour because he didn't know what would happen next. He remembered that when they entered the tunnel their heading was 290 degrees, but now the compass was spinning. Very soon they could be going in any direction, even right back into the dangerous cloud. But now he called upon his "visionary compass," an ability he had developed during the past couple of months, which could best be described as an intuitive sense of direction.

"I created an imaginary compass in my mind," Gernon said. "It was located just above my eyes and looked exactly like a magnetic compass, a drum-like scale, marked in degrees. It was about six inches in diameter and floated inside my skull. It always remained horizontal and pointed to true north no matter which direction I was facing. So I put my visionary compass to use to maintain a 290-degree heading."

Gernon's "internal compass" is an ability that is similar to a technique used by shamans in Indonesia, which was described by researcher John Perkins in his book *Psycho-Navigation: Techniques for Travel.* Perkins was shown the skill by present-day shamans among the Bugis of Indonesia, who still build wooden ships—as they have done for centuries—and cross great distances of open water with no compasses or other navigational tools.

At this point, Gernon and his two passengers had been traveling for nearly thirty-two minutes. According to their flight time, they should have been approaching the chain of Bimini Islands, which extend fifty-five miles south of Bimini, the main island, to Orange Cay, the southernmost island in the chain. He estimated that they were about ninety-five miles southwest of Miami, and just shy of twenty miles from crossing the Bimini chain. If his internal compass was working, Gernon figured they would be crossing the islands in six or seven minutes.

"Off to the right, we saw a dark area that looked like land, but it was too soon for the islands. I figured it was probably the shadow of a cloud rather than an island. Pilots often mistake such shadows for islands when flying in the Bahamas, especially when they're getting anxious to find a checkpoint. But as we flew past the dark spot, it seemed to go by us much too quickly. So I decided it must be a cloud moving in the opposite direction."

They continued on, still shrouded by the odd haze. Gernon was puzzled by the conditions, but the air was stable and he felt in control of the airplane. "We remained on the Miami frequency, but didn't hear any transmissions for several minutes, which seemed odd. Then, suddenly, we heard the voice of the controller, who yelled that he had spotted an airplane directly over Miami Beach, flying due west."

Time Distortion

Gernon looked at his watch and saw that they had been flying for just under thirty-four minutes. "We couldn't possibly be over Miami Beach yet, so I told the controller that we were approximately ninety miles southwest of Miami, and still looking for the Bimini Islands."

Suddenly, the fog started to break apart, but it didn't just dissipate. Long ribbons of fog ran parallel to their direction of flight. The ribbons spread apart until clear sky appeared as long slits in the fog. The ribbons were about one mile from the plane, and ran two-to-three miles in front of them, and about the same distance behind them. The slits gradually grew wider, and then, within several seconds, the slits all connected and the ribbons of fog disappeared.

"All I could see was brilliant blue sky, and then my eyes adjusted to the brightness, and I recognized Miami Beach directly below us."

The three men were relieved to see familiar land again and to have escaped the fog. For some reason, Gernon knew that it was important to remember the clouds that he'd seen. It was an odd thought, almost as if it had come from outside of him. "The clouds we'd gone through were certainly extraordinary, but I had no idea how or why they would be significant.

"Dad noticed that the navigation instruments appeared to be working again, so he used them to verify our position. I contacted the radar controller and told him that he was correct about our location over Miami Beach. I thanked him for his assistance and signed off the radio."

They headed north and skirted around a thunderstorm near Fort Lauderdale. After they landed at Palm Beach International, Gernon noticed that the flight had taken forty-seven minutes. "I thought something must be wrong with the plane's timer. But all three of our watches showed that it was 3:48 PM. The airplane clock showed the same time.

"I had made this flight from Palm Beach to Andros at least a dozen times and had never flown it in less than seventy-five minutes, and that was on a direct route. This flight was indirect and would probably cover a distance of close to two hundred and fifty miles. The Bonanza could not possibly travel that distance in forty-seven minutes when its maximum cruising speed was one hundred and ninety-five miles an hour. We had no answers."

Another year passed before Gernon learned about the legend of the Bermuda Triangle, and that his experience was part of a larger picture.

Who Drew
the Triangle?

It could be said that Christopher Columbus discovered the Bermuda Triangle—a statement that actually might be more accurate than the one about Columbus discovering America. We now know that other explorers preceded Columbus and, of course, the land had been inhabited for many thousands of years. But the arrival of Columbus in the New World definitely marked the beginning of a major shift in the Americas. At the time of the gradual invasion of the land populated by Native Americans, Europeans were entering the Renaissance, an era of science and reason. That essentially meant that the myths and legends of the Native Americans were doomed as the dominant belief pattern in America shifted to a time of discovery and conflict—and the beginning of recorded history in the Americas.

Columbus himself kept careful notes on his voyages into the Caribbean. His first baffling encounters took place in the Sargasso Sea. The crew expected to find land when they encountered seaweed and birds, but days went by and no land was sighted. Soon after, Columbus reported his compass acting strangely. Fearing that the deeply superstitious crew would rebel, he kept that information to himself.

However, he couldn't protect the crew from all the mysterious events taking place around them. At one point in his log, on that famous voyage of 1492, he described an enormous glowing ball of light, which hovered above the sea. Columbus and Pedro Gutierrez were on the deck of the Santa Maria when they observed "a light glimmering at a great distance." It vanished and reappeared several times during the night, moving up and down "in sudden and passing gleams."

Columbus didn't know what the light was, but he considered it a portent, a sign that they were being guided. Indeed, four hours after spotting the light, they glimpsed land for the first time.

The Origin of the Triangle

While unusual phenomena in the Caribbean has been noted from the time Columbus arrived, the first mention of the area as a center of mysterious disappearances was reported in an Associated Press dispatch by E.V.W. Jones in 1950. Two years later, an article by George X. Sand in *Fate* magazine restated the claim. But it wasn't until 1964, in the February issue of *Argosy* magazine, that writer/researcher Vincent Gaddis coined the term "Bermuda Triangle." The following year, he used it again in his book *Invisible Horizons*. The phrase took hold, even though the mystery is by no means restricted by rigid borders drawn on a map. In fact, many of the lost vessels and aircraft disappeared outside of the imaginary boundaries. One writer who mapped the disappearances called the mysterious area a "trapezium"—a rectangle in which no two sides or angles are the same. Yet, the word "triangle" seems to suggest something mysterious, something that pulls us into it.

Regardless of its shape, the Bermuda Triangle was not well known in December of 1970 when Gernon took off from Andros Island en route to West Palm Beach. At the time, he had never heard the term or anything about mysterious conditions in the Caribbean. But he knew that something unusual had happened to him and he vowed to remember every detail.

In the weeks before the flight, Gernon had been watching the acclaimed thirteen-part BBC television series *The Ascent of Man*. He had been particularly impressed by the description of how Leonardo da Vinci created one of his portraits. When da Vinci was a young man, he met a strikingly beautiful woman who made a powerful impression on him. He decided that one day he would paint her likeness, even though he never saw her again. According to the story, da Vinci spent ten or fifteen minutes two or three times a day painting a mental portrait of the woman. He did it every day for more than thirty years before he finally put paint on canvas. By that time, he had a perfect image of her as if she were seated in front of him posing for the portrait. The painting, of course, became one of his most famous works—the portrait of Mona Lisa.

It was this method of remembering that Gernon used to recall every detail of the flight on December 4, 1970. "I had never seen clouds like those before, so by using da Vinci's method, I was able to remember everything as if I'd made the flight yesterday."

At first, he didn't talk to anyone about the enigmatic flight because it didn't make sense. He didn't know how to explain it. "I couldn't figure it out, but I felt that something significant had happened, so I continued to review the flight several times every day for months."

Then, some fourteen months after the flight, Gernon saw Gaddis and another writer, Ivan Sanderson, on *The Dick Cavett Show* talking about a mysterious area of the Caribbean called the "Bermuda Triangle," or "Devil's Triangle." It was the first time he had heard either term. Sanderson was explaining some of the possible causes of the disappearances in the Caribbean, when he mentioned the possibility of a time warp.

"That was a momentous moment for me," Gernon recalled. "It was as if lightning bolts went off inside my head. I realized that time was the key to what had happened to us; that a time warp, of some sort, would account for our early arrival with too much gas. We flew into a tunnel in the cloud near Bimini and came out of the haze four minutes later near Miami, a hundred miles away—an impossible feat."

After the Cavett show, Gernon realized that he was part of a mysterious phenomenon, and he had survived. Within months, the Bermuda Triangle became a household term. During the early 1970s, a host of books were published about this navigational Twilight Zone, and for a few years tourism in the Caribbean faltered as people became wary about the region. The most popular of those books, *The Bermuda Triangle*, by Charles Berlitz (Doubleday), sold more than five million copies. A second book by Berlitz, *Without a Trace*, also sold well.

Other books on the phenomenon included *Encounters in the Devil's Triangle* by James Paul Chaplin (Zebra), *The Riddle of the Bermuda Triangle* by Martin Ebron (Signet), *The Bermuda Triangle* by Adi-Kent Thomas Jeffrey (Warner), *They Dared the Devil's Triangle* by Adi-Ken Thomas Jeffrey (Warner), *Secrets of the Bermuda Triangle* by Alan Landsbury (Warner), *The Devil's Sea* by Elizabeth Nichols, (Award), *Triangle of the Lost* by Warren Smith (Zebra), *Limbo of the Lost* by John Wallace Spencer (Bantam), *The Devil's Triangle* by Richard Winer (Bantam), followed by two sequels, and *Vanished Without a Trace* by Bill Wisner (Berkley).

Keeping Count

Imagine if the Bermuda Triangle were the stage for a master magician and all the famous disappearances were his magical effects. Some of the names of his greatest feats, besides the renowned Flight 19, would be the *Star Tiger* and the *Star Ariel.* The list goes on and on.

But magicians, the ones who can make elephants and pickup trucks disappear, also make them return and everyone applauds. Of course, that's not the case with the numerous ships and airplanes that have vanished in the Bermuda Triangle. Once they disappeared, they were gone. In some cases, the wreckage has been discovered. But in many others no remains were ever found.

It's impossible to know the exact number of ships and airplanes that have disappeared over the years. Certainly, their numbers far exceed the ones that were recorded. According to one publicized estimate made by the Discovery Channel in their investigation, more than eight thousand people have died in the Bermuda Triangle since 1851, and more than 150 airplanes have disappeared since 1930. It's much more difficult to count the ships that have vanished in the Bermuda Triangle. Many smaller noncommercial vessels vanish and their loss goes unrecorded. However, Gian Quasar of BermudaTriangle.org estimates that more than a thousand vessels have disappeared in just the last twenty-five years.

Taking Aim at the Triangle

But by the mid-1970s, debunkers appeared on the scene and began picking apart the disappearances of ships and planes, attributing them to storms, mechanical failures, and human error. The Bermuda Triangle was labeled a pseudo-mystery, as real as comic book tales of fantastic journeys to other worlds and hidden civilizations nestled inside a "hollow Earth." Even Lloyds of London took a position against the mystery when it reported that the Bermuda Triangle was statistically no more dangerous than any other region of the oceans. It didn't matter that they had failed to take into account that many disappearances in the Bermuda Triangle—vessels carrying refugees and drug-laden planes—are not reported. It was safe to go back in the Caribbean waters—or so it seemed.

The most well-known work debunking the mystery was *The Bermuda Triangle Mystery—Solved* by Lawrence Kusche (New English Library), published in 1975. A librarian at Arizona State University, Kusche compiled *The Bermuda Triangle Bibliography,* a collection of reference materials about lost vessels and aircraft in the Caribbean. Kusche said he found the books on the Bermuda Triangle sensational and complained that Berlitz and other writers didn't stick to the facts.

Ironically, Berlitz and others used Kusche's bibliography as a resource for their books. So, Kusche actually was the source of some of the best-known stories. In fact, in early editions of his book, Berlitz praised the librarian in the introduction to his bibliography. "Before mention of some of the books referred to in this present work, the author would like to recommend to the reader's attention the *Bermuda Triangle Bibliography*, compiled by Larry Kusche and Deborah Blouin, Arizona State University Library, April 1973, which contains numerous references, including books and newspaper and magazine articles, pertaining to the Bermuda Triangle."

Because Kusche's book was billed as an effort to straighten the record and to put to rest any nonsense about mysterious and unknown forces in the Bermuda Triangle, readers might have assumed that it was authoritative and accurate. It wasn't.

Kusche relied heavily on newspaper accounts, assuming they were correct when the information supported him, and wrong when they didn't. One researcher, who has studied Kusche's book as well as Berlitz and others, found inaccuracies on both sides of the issue. "There are no more mistakes in Charles Berlitz's book *The Bermuda Triangle* than there are in Larry Kusche's book *The Bermuda Triangle Mystery—Solved*. Berlitz had inaccurate information upon which he based aspects of the theories. So did Larry Kusche for his solution," wrote Gian Quasar, whose detailed website on the Bermuda Triangle surpasses all other Internet attempts to examine the mystery.

Whenever newspaper articles and other sources didn't support Kusche's assumptions, he rejected them. Regarding the disappearance of the USS *Cyclops*, Kusche wrote: "I confidently decided that the newspapers, the Navy, and all the ships at sea had been wrong, and that there had been a storm near Norfolk that day strong enough to sink the ship." Later, he added: "Contrary to popular opinion, there never was an official inquiry into the disappearance. Had there been any investigation, the weather information would surely have been discovered."

As a matter of fact, three boxes (numbers 1068–1070) at the National Archives contain 1,500 papers on the official investigation into the disappearance of the USS *Cyclops*. There is no mention of the storm that Kusche is so confident about.

Kusche's title is somewhat deceptive and sensationalistic in its own right. Rather than solving the mystery of the Bermuda Triangle, he ends a number of his investigations admitting that there is indeed a mystery. In the case of the *Mary Celeste*, a derelict ship found in the Atlantic, he concluded: "Today the fate of the occupants of the *Mary Celeste* is as much a mystery as the day the ship was found deserted at sea."

In the case of the *Star Tiger*, his comments sound similar. "In any case, whatever happened to the *Star Tiger* will forever remain a mystery." And again on another investigation: "The fate of *Joshua Slocum* and the *Spray* is truly a mystery of the sea."

Gernon admits that Kusche may be right in his assumption that some of the disappearances of airplanes were caused by human error. But Kusche didn't know that an unknown meteorological phenomenon may very well have caused pilots to make those errors. "If Kusche had been my copilot on the day I flew through the electromagnetic storm and into the electronic fog, I'm sure his viewpoint on the Bermuda Triangle wouldn't be so wrongheaded."

The Mystery That Won't Disappear

By the 1980s and '90s, even some authors of books speculating on mysteries such as UFOs, Bigfoot, and other unknown phenomenon, had followed Kusche's lead and downgraded the Bermuda Triangle to the level of a false rumor. For example, author Jerome Clark in *Unexplained!* labeled the Bermuda Triangle a non-mystery and wrote what sounded like its obituary. "The once famous Bermuda Triangle survives only as a footnote in the history of fads and passing sensations."

It seemed a safe thing to say. But he was wrong. So was Kusche. Something *is* out there, literally moving below our radar, and it won't go away. We can't see it, but we can sense it. And, if the television documentaries are any indication, we want to know more.

Cable networks running old documentaries on the Bermuda Triangle, saw high ratings. They began sending out teams of documentary filmmakers, and found that the mystery wasn't dead at all, merely dormant. By the approach of the millennium, the Bermuda Triangle was awakening again, rising like the mythical phoenix from its own ashes. The mystery returned to popular consciousness and found new life, especially among the millions who were too young to remember its heyday during the 1970s. The new documentaries were broadcast on the Discovery Channel, the History Channel, TLC (The Learning Channel), the Travel Channel, and PAX. The continual productions and the repeat show-ings were testimonials that there was interest in the mystery.

The reason for all the attention is simple. Baffling things happen in the Bermuda Triangle. While many of the mysterious disappearances took place long ago, new cases are reported on a regular basis. We'll focus next on airplanes lost at sea in recent years.

Updates from the Triangle

The name evokes a legend, an aura of mystery, a watery realm harboring a secret, a place that exists more in myth than in reality. Over the past thirty years, the Bermuda Triangle has become part of the folklore of the sea and the air, a region where at any moment a mysterious fog might cling to a vessel like tight clothing, where the navigational instruments might fail, where ships, planes, and people simply vanish.

Things are still happening in the Bermuda Triangle. Pilots encounter strange fogs that don't register on radar, electronic instruments go haywire, disoriented pilots nosedive to their deaths, and on occasion, the occupants of an aircraft experience a time distortion.

Take the case of a Piper on a flight from the Bahamas to West Palm Beach, Florida, during the early morning of July 20, 2002. The six-seat Piper Lance II took off from the Freeport International Airport in the Bahamas at 5:35 AM. Within a few minutes, the craft reached 4,700 feet, and the pilot switched radio contact from Freeport to the Miami air traffic control.

The plane fell off the radar twenty-five minutes after take-off and crashed fifteen miles off the north coast of Grand Bahama Island. Although rain clouds were forming that morning, there were no dangerous thunderstorms in the area. The rented Piper was twenty-four years old, but it had recently undergone a major overhaul that cost $60,000 and included a new engine and new electronics. "There was nothing wrong with that plane," Michael Callegio, owner of the Piper, said after the accident.

The pilot, Craig Huber, an Air Force veteran, had 280 hours of flying time, and had spent four hours in the air with a flight trainer at the Palm Beach Flight Training School before the school rented the plane to him. "It was clear he knew what he was doing," Tara Palmer, the school's office manager, told a *Palm Beach Post* reporter.

Investigators focused on the fact that Huber wasn't licensed to fly in the dark, using only instruments, and that the plane had taken off from the Bahamas an hour before sunrise. However, dawn was approaching at the time of the crash and the sky should have been light enough to see by unless the plane was locked in fog. Investigators also suggested that a night of gambling that had continued into the early morning hours might have affected the pilot's decisionmaking abilities.

Since there were no survivors, it will never be known whether or not the Piper's electronic instruments suddenly failed or acted oddly as the plane entered a strange fog, as is the case in some of the mysterious happenings in the Bermuda Triangle. However, the location of the crash raises other questions.

Why was the plane fifteen miles *north* of the island, 90 degrees off course, when it should have been flying due east toward West Palm Beach? Also, where did the plane go during the flight? The Piper should have traveled at least forty-five miles during its twenty-five minutes in the air.

At a minimal climbing rate of 500 feet per minute, it would take just over nine minutes to reach 4,700 feet. During that time the Piper would travel about fifteen miles. That leaves another fifteen minutes of flying time and at least thirty miles unaccounted for prior to the crash.

Confusion, disorientation, and repeated turns could account for the location of the plane at the time of the crash. If the plane were swallowed by electronic fog after taking off, the instruments might have failed. The pilot would be confused and disoriented. He would make repeated turns that might account for some of the missing miles. However, a time distortion caused by the fog might also account for the missing miles. If the plane moved backward in time fifteen minutes, that would explain the lack of distance traveled.

Coworkers at Palm Beach National Golf and Country Club, where Huber was the head golf pro, called him an extremely competent pilot and known for his smooth landings. "He's been piloting too long to do something dumb," Tim McArthur, a friend and golfing partner, told the *Post*.

But one of the passengers might have sensed that this would be his last flight into the Bermuda Triangle, or anywhere. Chuck Anderson called his mother shortly before leaving on the flight to the Bahamas and said, "I just want everybody to know I love them in case I don't come back."

Then he called a friend and gave him a similar message. "It was surreal, almost like he had a premonition," the friend recalled a couple of days after the crash.

––––––––––––––

Another mysterious airplane crash, involving a Piper, occurred off the Florida Keys on February 1, 2001, when an experienced private pilot encountered a fog and abruptly nose-dived into the ocean. At the time of the incident, Casey Purvis, a successful South Florida businessman, was working as a volunteer in a training program with the U.S. Coast Guard Auxiliary. Purvis and copilot Rob Fuller were posing as drug smugglers entering the country for coast guard pilots in training.

Just before the crash, the lead pilot for the coast guard, who was flying a coast guard Falcon jet, was moving south over the Everglades at an altitude of one-thousand feet. About half a mile ahead of them, Purvis was flying his Piper Archer 32-300 at fifteen-hundred feet. As the plane approached the ranger station in Flamingo, Purvis was asked if he was comfortable continuing an additional two or three miles. He said that was "no problem," and that he could see the Marathon airport about twenty-five miles to the south.

However, a minute or so later, Purvis reported that he was surrounded by a haze. The coast guard plane turned north and the crew asked Purvis to follow at a slower pace, so they could get greater distance between them for another intercept. He responded that he was flying by instruments and that he would continue flying in a southerly direction.

The Falcon jet crew informed Purvis that they were well ahead of him in clear weather and there was no conflict with their craft. A short time later they called Purvis again, but this time he didn't answer. Several more calls were made, and when there was no response, a search was launched for the missing pilot.

In spite of the coast guard's request to turn north, Purvis continued flying to the south. According to the radar data, the Piper was southbound at sixteen-hundred feet at 7:47 PM. For the next several minutes, the plane made slight maneuvers first right, then left, for a total of seven unexplained turns. The plane dropped to fifteen-hundred feet, and then vanished from the radar at 7:51 PM.

Purvis was an avid volunteer in the auxiliary program and often flew twenty to thirty hours per week for the group. He had a spotless flying record with no accidents, incidents, or violations. He had recorded 1,586 hours of flight time, including 1,375 of them in the Piper. He'd flown one hundred and forty-nine hours at night and sixty-five hours flying by instruments, and he was instrument rated. He'd worked with the coast guard for more than two years.

When the plane was recovered from six feet of water, the National Transportation Safety Board (NTSB) found no evidence of mechanical failure or faulty instruments. The pilot's son reported that the gas tank of the plane had been filled before takeoff. Even though Purvis had reported fog and poor visibility, weather conditions at the time were clear, with a visibility of nine miles and light winds.

The NTSB concluded that Purvis had become spatially disoriented, was unable to tell which way was up, and flew into the ocean. The report stated: "Lack of natural horizon or such reference is common on over-water flights, and especially at night in sparsely populated areas, or in low-visibility conditions. The disoriented pilot may place the aircraft in a dangerous attitude. Therefore, the use of flight instruments is essential to maintain proper attitude when encountering any of the elements, which may result in spatial disorientation."

Yet as noted above, Purvis was experienced at flying in such conditions. He had flown frequently at night and also was comfortable using only instruments. However, if the instruments had temporarily failed as a result of electromagnetic anomalies, that situation would offer a better explanation about why Purvis flew his plane into the sea.

It happened far from the Bermuda Triangle, but there are some interesting similarities between the crash of the Piper flown by John F. Kennedy, Jr., and the one piloted by Casey Purvis. The Kennedy crash, on a flight en route to Martha's Vineyard, received more attention and scrutiny than any other crash by a private plane.

The flight originated on July 16, 1999, at Essex County Airport, where Kennedy notified the tower of his plan to takeoff. No further communication was heard from the plane at either Essex or at Martha's Vineyard.

Although the tower in Martha's Vineyard was reporting clear weather conditions and visibility between eight and ten miles, three pilots who flew to the island that same evening reported hazy conditions with visibility restricted to three-to-five miles. None of the pilots reported clouds or fog.

One pilot said that, as he flew over Martha's Vineyard on a descent from 17,500 feet, he couldn't see the island. "There was nothing to see. There was no horizon and no light. . . . I turned left toward Martha's Vineyard to see if it was visible, but could see no lights of any kind nor any evidence of the island. I thought the island might have suffered a power failure." Another pilot canceled his flight to Martha's Vineyard because of poor weather. "From my own judgment, visibility appeared to be approximately four miles—extremely hazy."

Like Purvis, Kennedy apparently became confused and disoriented and began a series of turns that led to the crash. About thirty-four miles west of Martha's Vineyard, the radar indicated that the plane began a descent from fifty-five-hundred feet. At about 9:38 PM, the Piper banked to the right for five minutes while making a steady descent to twenty-two-hundred feet, then started climbing to twenty-five-hundred feet as it finished the turn.

Two minutes later, the plane entered a left turn, making a 28-degree bank, and climbed to twenty-six-hundred feet. After fifteen seconds, it began descending rapidly at nine hundred feet per minute and banked to the right again at a 45-degree angle. The plane continued banking and entered a "death spiral" as it increased its descent speed to more than forty-seven-hundred feet per minute, until it collided with the water at about 9:41 PM.

The turns, however, were not the only evidence that Kennedy was disoriented. To avoid a death spiral, he should have throttled back, slowing the plane as much as possible. But the investigators analyzing the wreckage found that the throttle and propeller controls were set at full forward.

In both the Kennedy and Purvis cases, the National Transportation Safety Board concluded that spatial disorientation was the cause of the crash. While Kennedy wasn't as experienced as Purvis, he had passed the FAA's written airplane instrument exam, and his instructor rated him as having "very good" flying skills for his level of experience. He said that Kennedy's basic instrument flying skills and simulator work were excellent.

Since Kennedy never called the tower in Martha's Vineyard, it's unknown what conditions he experienced. The NTSB report concluded that Kennedy became disoriented in the hazy conditions even though other pilots flew through the same conditions that night without incident. But like Purvis, it's possible that Kennedy entered a more severe condition, a localized fog, not reported by the weather service, the tower, or other pilots. It could have been electronic fog, associated with electromagnetic radiation, and it could have created low visibility rather than the reported condition. It also could have affected the electronic and magnetic navigational instruments.

But we'll never know.

One of the strangest and most documented cases of an airplane's sudden and dramatic disappearance involved a short flight from St. Croix to St. Thomas by a charter plane. In 1978, Eastern Caribbean Flight 912 simply disappeared in good weather as it was about to land at the St. Thomas airport.

"The pilot contacted me on the final approach when he was about fifteen miles south of the airport," recalled William Kittenger, who was an air traffic controller at St. Thomas airport. Nothing seemed out of the ordinary. "Then when he was two miles out, I had visual contact."

Kittenger looked away as he cleared another flight for take-off. When he peered out again expecting to see the Najavo approaching the runway, he couldn't see it. He checked the radar; the plane was gone. "I figured the plane was down. I called the crash crew and coast guard immediately. They were on the scene within minutes."

Even though Flight 912 crashed in shallow water, there was no wreckage found, no bodies, no debris, not even a signal from its electronic tracking device. It was as if the plane had vanished into thin air. Kittenger, who was interviewed for a recent documentary on the Discovery Channel, is still baffled by the incident. "It would have to leave some sort of debris. If you pushed a large object off the top of a 1,000-foot-high building into shallow water, it would leave some sort of debris."

But nothing was ever found.

Sometimes planes vanish in perfectly clear weather. On June 5, 1990, a Cherokee 150 disappeared in clear skies and calm seas as it approached St. Croix in the U.S. Virgin Islands. Mary Pomeroy, a British citizen, took off at 3:12 PM. from St. Maarten, Netherlands Antilles. At 3:19 PM, she contacted the San Juan, Puerto Rico, tower and reported her flight plan. A few minutes later, she radioed again, saying: "Zero, two, foxtrot four-five at the boundary, over." The message indicated that she was entering U.S. airspace. That was the last that was heard from Pomeroy.

When the plane failed to appear at the St. Croix airport, a search was undertaken. A coast guard cutter *Chilula* coordinated the effort with a British Virgin Islands's police boat, another coast guard cutter, a helicopter, and two C-130 Hercules. They covered 7,500 miles of calm seas over two days without finding a trace of the plane, which was equipped with several floatation devices, including an orange liferaft. Even more puzzling, searchers detected no signals from either of the emergency location transmitters onboard. That could mean that other electronic equipment also failed. The report by the National Transportation Safety Board lists the cause as undetermined, and the case remains unsolved.

It was a clear evening on January 5, 2000, when a Cessna 172 approached the St. Augustine airport in northern Florida. At 9:42 PM, the pilot was identified on radar as three miles south of St. Augustine, flying inland over the Intracoastal Waterway at 2,600 feet. Three minutes later, the air traffic controller spotted him on radar at 2,000 feet as he continued his northerly heading.

The pilot, en route to Jacksonville, should have continued following the coast. However, during the next thirty seconds, the plane made a right turn and descended to 1,200 feet. Then, when he was about two miles offshore and heading east, the pilot spoke to the controller again. This time he sounded nervous.

"I don't have a direction finder. I don't see anything."

"Say again," the controller answered after about thirty seconds. The pilot didn't respond. Seconds later, the plane vanished from radar. The body and pieces of the plane were recovered four miles offshore the next day.

The report by the National Transportation Safety Board attributed the crash to spatial disorientation by the pilot. "The pilot's lack of experience in instrument flight resulted in the pilot becoming spatially disoriented, and the subsequent collision with water. Contributing to the accident was the dark night, with no visible horizon."

But why did the pilot abruptly turn out to sea and why couldn't he find the brightly lit coast again? One possible answer is that he entered a patch of dense localized fog and never escaped. Still, he could have followed his compass, turned west, and returned to the coast, unless his compass began to spin and his instruments failed. In that case, with no sign of a horizon or city lights, confusion and disorientation would have sent him quickly into a death spiral.

Many similar cases are found in the files of the National Transportation Safety Board. For example, John Potter and a friend took off from St. Croix in a Cessna 150 on a clear day in late June 1979. They planned a short flight to St. Thomas for a three-day vacation. The flight was airborne at 5:11 PM, and six minutes later Potter contacted the St. Croix tower requesting a routine frequency change. But that was the last anyone heard from the pilot. The plane never arrived in St. Thomas, and no trace of the plane or passengers was ever found.

While the crash of a commercial airliner or a private plane carrying a well-known person such as John Kennedy, Jr., gathers significant media coverage, most private planes that disappear from radar above the Bermuda Triangle and are never seen again, receive little or no public notice. Besides the recorded cases, there are many disappearances that never reach the public, and are never recorded at all. For example, pilots of some noncommercial aircraft sometimes don't file flight plans. Among them are planes carrying illegal drugs into the country. When they fail to arrive at their destination, either no one knows about it or, if anyone does, it's not reported.

One little-known case involved an Aero Commander 500B that crashed off Nassau on May 12, 1999, under good flying conditions. At the time of the accident, the pilot was in radio contact with Nassau Approach Control. For some reason, the pilot made a 360-degree turn without permission and was then directed to runway nine. None of the radio communications indicated that the pilot was having mechanical or medical problems. The pilot acknowledged that he was about to land on the specified runway. Then the plane dove into the sea. All that was found were an empty six-man life raft, five yellow life jackets, and a few small pieces of the plane.

While NTSB indicated that pilot error was the likely cause of the crash, again the matter remains open. Was the plane caught in a localized fog during the final approach? Did the instruments fail, as if seized by a magnetic anomaly? With no survivor and no wreckage, the answer will never be known.

––––––––––––

Such a fog was blamed for a minor crash at the St. John's airport in St. Augustine on January 18, 2001. A student pilot was completing a supervised solo cross-country flight when the incident occurred. During the landing, the plane veered off the left side of the runway and collided with an airport sign. The pilot explained that just before landing he was shrouded in fog and lost sight of the runway. He touched down safely, then angled off the runway.

The problem with the pilot's explanation was that the fog was so localized that no one else saw it. Weather conditions were clear with a ten-mile visibility and witnesses at the airport didn't notice any fog either. It sounds as if the student pilot simply made up an excuse for his mistake. But considering the elusive nature of electronic fog, there may be reason to give the pilot the benefit of the doubt.

Here's the case of a flight from Florida to Cuba that never arrived at its destination; no trace of the aircraft was ever found.

Argosy Airlines, a Caribbean charter line, was hired by twenty-one American citrus growers in the fall of 1978 to fly them to Florida from Havana at the end of their tour of the country. Special permission was obtained for Flight 902, since Cuba is restricted territory.

The plane left Fort Lauderdale at midday under partly cloudy skies. After reaching 6,000 feet, pilot George Hamilton called Miami Center. Oddly, there was no response. Awhile later, at 12:25 PM, the Argosy contacted Havana, but static interference made messages from the Argosy indecipherable. As a courtesy, a high-altitude plane relayed the messages to Havana. At 12:35 PM, the messages became loud and clear.

Havana was ready to guide it in. Havana radar showed the Argosy to the right of its course. Then, just minutes later, at 12:43 PM, Argosy Flight 902 was gone. There was no more green blip on the scope. There was no SOS. There was no ELT signal.

Miami and Havana coordinated an immediate search. USAF and U.S. Coast Guard units raced to the scene, while Cuban air patrol made overflights within the hour. By afternoon, coast guard cutter *Steadfast* was coordinating the surface effort. The search was expanded to all traffic, plus four more cutters, a helicopter, and a C-131.

The following cable was sent out:

ALL SHIPPING STRAITS OF FLORIDA-NICHOLAS
CHANNEL ARGOSY AIRLINES FLT. 902 (N407D)
IS OVERDUE ON A FLIGHT FROM FORT
LAUDERDALE TO HAVANA, CUBA. DESC: WHITE
WITH BLUE TRIM. 4 PERSONS ON BOARD. ALL
SHIPS ARE REQUESTED TO KEEP A SHARP
LOOKOUT FOR DEBRIS, YELLOW LIFE JACKETS.
PEOPLE IN THE WATER. SIGNED U.S. COAST
GUARD, MIAMI, FL.

The DC-3 carried thirty-two yellow life jackets, as well as floatable seat cushions. But nothing was ever found; no debris. The plane and crew of four had vanished. The National Transportation and Safety Board report concluded that weather conditions shouldn't have interfered with the flight: "Weather data available for the time and place of the aircraft's last identified radar position revealed that circumnavigation of the weather cells should have presented no problem, and probably accounts for the slight deviation of the flight to the right of course."

Pilot error was also discounted when it was discovered that Hamilton had amassed 15,227 total flight hours, 3,000 in DC-3s. The case was closed with no speculation on the reason for the plane's disappearance.

The cases go on and on. Some of the disappearances certainly may be ordinary—bad weather, bad equipment, or bad decisionmaking. But others hold mysterious and inexplicable elements that suggest the working of an anomalous force, which might emanate either from the air, the sea, or even the earth below the sea. In the next chapter, we'll take a closer look at the best known and one of the most mysterious cases, the controversial Flight 19.

Flight to Oblivion

Nothing else in the legend of the Bermuda Triangle has attracted as much interest and stirred so much controversy as the saga of Flight 19. The story of five Navy planes with a crew of fourteen airmen, who couldn't find the continental United States from the nearby Bahamas, has baffled generations. The squadron vanished without a trace and was followed into oblivion by one of the search crafts.

If Flight 19 had returned home safely, the Bermuda Triangle might never have gained its boundaries, its name, and its notoriety. It would be regarded as an area where strange things sometimes happened, an area of deadly storms and puzzling electromagnetic anomalies that caused equipment failures. But in the years following the loss of Flight 19, researchers gathered stories of other lost planes and boats and noted a confluence of disappearances. They labeled the unlucky area of sea and air as the "Devil's Triangle," the "Hoodoo Triangle," and, as previously mentioned, the Bermuda Triangle.

It began the early afternoon of December 5, 1945, as five Avenger torpedo bombers departed the Fort Lauderdale Naval

Air Station on a routine training mission. The route formed a triangle: east to the Berry Islands, then north to an island near Grand Bahama Island, then back to Fort Lauderdale. Two similar squadrons had completed the exercise earlier in the day and another one had left just twenty-five minutes ahead of Flight 19. None of the other squadrons experienced any difficulties. This flight, however, would turn into something extraordinary. The lead pilot would become disoriented, his compasses would fail, and he would become convinced that they were impossibly off course. All five planes and all fourteen airmen would vanish without a trace.

The first sign of trouble was recorded at 3:40 PM, an hour and a half after takeoff. Lieutenant Robert Cox, a senior instructor at the naval air station, who was also flying at the time, overheard Lieutenant Charles Taylor, the flight commander, asking his second-in-command for help on the squadron's assigned radio frequency. Cox later told the naval board of investigators that Taylor kept asking Marine Captain Edward J. Powers, Jr. what his compass read. Finally, Taylor admitted he was lost. "I don't know where we are. We must have got lost after that last turn."

Cox contacted Taylor on the radio and asked what was wrong. Taylor replied: "Both my compasses are out and I'm trying to find Fort Lauderdale. I'm over land, but it's broken. I'm sure I'm in the keys, but I don't know how far down and I don't know how to get to Fort Lauderdale."

In retrospect, it seems that something was affecting Taylor's thinking as well as his instruments. Taylor had been based in Key West and was familiar with the area. Any pilot with even a fraction of his experience flying in the keys would know that to reach Fort Lauderdale would simply require following the chain of islands to the mainland with the afternoon sun to the rear and left of the plane.

Cox told Taylor to put the sun on his port wing and fly up the coast until he reached Fort Lauderdale. "What's your present altitude? I'll fly down and meet you."

After a moment, Taylor replied: "I know where I am now. I'm at 2,300 feet. Don't come after me."

"Roger, you're at 2300. I'm coming to meet you anyhow," Cox answered.

Although four of the five pilots of Flight 19 were students in a training program, they were all experienced with an average of 400 hours of flying time. Their next assignment was to start landing on aircraft carriers, a task reserved for the Navy's more capable pilots. At twenty-nine, Taylor was the senior pilot. He had accumulated 2,509 flight hours and was considered an excellent pilot. But that day nothing seemed to go right for Taylor.

While Cox headed south toward the keys, he heard Taylor again on the radio: "Can you have Miami or someone turn on their radar gear and pick us up? We don't seem to be getting far."

Taylor also indicated that one of the students apparently had led the squadron. "We were out on a navigation hop, and the second leg I thought they were going wrong, so I took over and was flying back to the right position, but I'm sure now that neither one of my compasses is working."

Cox contacted Taylor again, and this time Taylor wasn't at all certain of his location. He kept asking the other pilots in the squadron for compass headings, but the confusion remained.

It seemed that none of the pilots was certain that their compasses were working. But is it possible that all of the compasses were malfunctioning?

Two decades later, as interest in the Bermuda Triangle peaked, the navy issued a report on Flight 19 that appeared in the June 1974 issue of *Sealift*. In it, Howard L. Rosenberg writes: "If the planes were flying through a magnetic storm, all compasses could possibly malfunction. Actually, man's knowledge of magnetism is limited. We know how to live with it and escape it by going into space, but we really don't know what exactly it is."

Cox told Taylor to turn on his emergency IFF gear, which, when activated, brightens the image on land-based radar screens. Taylor, in his confusion, at first said that he didn't have an IFF. But later he located it and turned it on. Cox also told Taylor to turn on his ZBX, a homing device much like the automatic direction finders used in planes today, which tells the pilot which direction to steer. Three land-based naval operations also radioed Taylor telling him to turn on his ZBX. None received a reply.

At 4:00 PM, Cox heard Taylor say that he was flying at forty-five-hundred feet, and visibility was ten-to-twelve miles. But the radio transmissions were fading and Cox was unable to contact Taylor again. Cox returned to Fort Lauderdale at 4:40 PM. under worsening weather conditions, as a storm moved in from the Atlantic. Cox heard one final transmission from Taylor in which he again said that he had assumed the lead of the flight after the student pilots had headed in the wrong direction.

In studying Flight 19, Bruce Gernon recreated the flight path followed by the squadron. The second checkpoint for the pilots was an island called Great Sale Cay, located about twenty miles north of Grand Bahama Island. Since they were heading north and the wind was increasing in intensity, they probably missed the island, passing it by ten miles to the east. That's when Taylor, who thought he was in the keys and about to reach Miami, radioed that "we don't seem to be getting far."

Years after his own experience in the Triangle, Gernon and his copilot Chris Hope flew a route similar to the one that Flight 19 had taken. Both pilots, who had lived in the Florida Keys, were amazed by the similarities between the Bahamas and the keys. Hope pointed out that one of the islands looked identical to Key Largo. They viewed the islands from different altitudes and the lower they went, the more they seemed to resemble the keys. In particular, a group of twenty islands between Grand Bahama and Little Abaco Island, known as the Cross Cays, looked like the islands in the lower keys surrounding Big Pine Key. The difference, of course, was that a series of bridges connect a string of keys. However, there are dozens of smaller keys that aren't connected by bridges.

When Lieutenant Commander Charles M. Kenyon, station operations officer of the Fort Lauderdale Naval Air Station, learned about Flight 19's problems, he wasn't overly concerned. Several other pilots had become disoriented in the past, and they'd all managed to find their way back to the base. Also, he'd recently lectured pilots on procedures to follow when planes become lost. He later told investigators: "I figured they were temporarily confused and with all the instructions we had given them, and with another plane in the air that had picked up the transmissions, they would come back right on time."

At 4:25, personnel at the Port Everglades Radio picked up a transmission from Taylor. "We've just passed over a small island. We have no other land in sight. I'm at altitude 3,500 feet. Have on emergency IFF. Does anyone in the area have a radar screen that could pick us up?"

At this point, Gernon thinks the squadron was passing over the barrier islands beyond Great Abaco Island. The islands are about ten miles apart, so they could fly for a short time without seeing land.

At about 4:30, Port Everglades Radio made contact with Taylor again. Since Taylor was having problems with his compass, they suggested that he let one of the other pilots lead the way back. Taylor acknowledged the suggestion, then a few minutes later he said that one of the pilots thought if they headed west, they would reach the mainland.

At 4:45, Taylor contacted Port Everglades and said: "We're heading 030 degrees for forty-five minutes; then we will fly north to make sure we are not over the Gulf of Mexico."

At about 5:00 PM, one of the student pilots told Taylor: "If we just fly west, we would get home." Another of the student pilots agreed. "Damn it, if we would just fly west. . . ."

But Taylor still believed they were over the Gulf of Mexico. He was heard telling the pilots to continue north for ten minutes. Then several minutes later he said: "We're going too damn far north instead of east. If there is anything, we would've seen it."

Then Taylor radioed the mainland again. "Hello, Port Everglades, this is Flight 19. Do you read? Over."

"Flight 19, this is Port Everglades. Go ahead."

"I receive you very weak. We are now heading west," he reported at 5:15.

At about that time, Taylor was heard telling all the planes to join up and continue in formation. If any plane had to ditch, they would all ditch together. Five minutes later, he said: "When the first man gets down to ten gallons of gas, we will all land in the water together. Does everyone understand that?"

Taylor's comments show his continued confusion and his growing anxiety. He was already talking about ditching in deep water. Yet they should have had more than two hours of fuel left, more than enough to make it back to the land they had flown over. But the sun was setting in about ten minutes. It was cloudy and there would be no moon.

"Port Everglades, this is Taylor. I receive you very weak. How is the weather over Lauderdale?"

"Weather over Lauderdale is clear. Over Key West CAVU (ceiling and visibility unlimited). Over the Bahamas—cloudy, rather low ceiling, poor visibility."

It would be pitch black outside the cockpit within half an hour. It was cloudy so there would be no moon and no stars. The ocean was rough because of the strong winds. Why they continued flying over deep water, instead of returning to the land that they'd seen within the last hour, was baffling. If they ditched in shallow water near shore, they would have a strong chance of surviving.

At about 6:00 PM, Port Everglades called Taylor. "Did you receive my last transmission. Change to 3000 kilocycles."

"Repeat once again."

"Change to channel one, 3000 kilocycles."

"I cannot change frequency," Taylor replied. "I must keep my planes intact. Cannot change to 3000 kilocycles, will stay on 4805 kilocycles."

Once again, Taylor was forgetting his training. An important part of the lost plane procedure is to change to the emergency frequency. The transmissions would come over the radio stronger, and there would be many more stations on the ground that would be able to hear them and be capable of replying and offering assistance. Taylor should have switched to the emergency frequency two hours earlier.

By 6:00, Flight 19 had been heading west for approximately forty-five minutes. When they made the turn, they were probably about ninety miles east-northeast of the barrier islands of the Abacos that they had mistaken for the Florida Keys. Now their location would be about fifty miles north of Walkers Cay, the northernmost Bahama Island. They would be just over a hundred miles off the Florida coast and would be able to reach the coastline in less than one hour.

By 6:02, Port Everglades was picking up fragments of conversations between the pilots. But none of the pilots could hear their calls.

"We may have to ditch at any moment," a voice said.

"Taylor to Powers. Do you read? . . .Taylor to Powers. I've been trying to reach you. Holding west course."

But then in another puzzling development, Taylor reverses himself again. "We didn't go far enough east. Turn around again. We may just as well turn around and go east again. . . . This is Taylor. Turn around and fly east until we run out of gas. I think we would have a better chance of being picked up close to shore."

"Taylor, this is Port Everglades. Do you read me?"

Unidentified voice: "Negative. . . . What course are we on? We are over the Gulf. We didn't go far enough east. . . . How long have we been on this course?"

Snatches of conversation were heard in the following minutes.

"Taylor to Powers. What is your course?"

Unidentified voice: "What course are we on now?"

After 6:17, only garbled transmissions were heard. Their voices became weaker and, by 7:04 PM, Flight 19 was silent.

At the time Taylor suggested they turn east again, the squadron would have been about seventy miles east of Florida. By that time it was dark, with a broken cloud ceiling from eight-hundred to twelve-hundred feet, with scattered showers. The wind was picking up out of the west-southwest gusting to thirty miles per hour. They would have been over the Gulf Stream, where the waves were building on the rough seas.

If they had maintained their westerly heading, they would have reached Florida before 7 PM. Unfortunately, they apparently took Taylor's bizarre suggestion to fly east until they ran out of gas. They would have vanished into the abyss of the Sargasso Sea.

Five navy seaplanes were dispatched shortly after 6:00. About ten ships in the search area were also alerted. Minutes earlier, ComGulf Sea Frontier Evaluation Center in Miami had vectored the approximate position of Flight 19. To obtain this position, the center used directional bearings that were sent from stations along the coastline from New Jersey to Texas. The position fix was quoted as being within a hundred-mile radius of 29 degrees, 15 minutes north, 79 degrees, 00 minutes west. Gernon believes the squadron was in the lower part of the south-southeastern quadrant of the area, about ninety miles east-northeast of the barrier islands of the Abacos, which Taylor had mistaken for the keys.

The search planes were handicapped by the darkness and storm conditions. No trace of the five Avengers was found, and one of the search planes vanished. No bodies were ever found, but one of the search ships saw an explosion that was probably the seaplane. Pieces of the wreckage were spotted, but conditions were too rough to recover any of it.

The next day, one of the largest searches in history started at sunrise. More than two hundred planes and seventeen ships joined the search for the missing airmen. The search area extended three hundred miles east into the Atlantic and north and south along the entire state. By sunset, no trace of Flight 19 had been found. The next day, two hundred and forty-two planes continued the search and additional ships joined those already prowling the seas for the lost squadron. Again, nothing was found. The effort continued for three more days.

On the fifth day, at 3:27 PM, a message was sent from Miami to all the planes, ships, and stations. "Search for five missing planes of December 5, 1945, will be terminated on completion of the return of all planes on the mission today. No further special search is contemplated. All planes and vessels in the area keep a bright lookout and report any pertinent information."

The search for Flight 19 was over. The men were all assumed dead. But the controversy about the reasons for the disappearance was just beginning.

———————

In January 1946, the Miami Naval Board of Investigation issued its final report on the case. "The primary reason for the disappearance of Flight 19 was the confusion of the flight leader as to his location, his failure to take into account the strong winds, which apparently carried him farther east than he realized, and his failure to utilize radio aids which were available to him."

Rear Admiral F. D. Wagner added a final note to the report: "The leaders of the flight became so hopelessly confused as to have suffered something akin to a mental aberration."

Charles Taylor's mother, Katherine Taylor, and her sister, Mary Carroll, were unhappy with the board's final report. They started a campaign urging the board to reconsider their decision to place the blame on Lieutenant Taylor. To that end, the sisters located a young attorney named William L. P. Burke. He was the ideal lawyer to defend the defamed pilot. The reason? Taylor had saved Burke's life twice while they were stationed together in Key West. The first time, Taylor flew a seaplane into the Bahamas and landed in a storm to save Burke, who was adrift on a life raft after a crash. Later, when Burke lost his way during a night flight, Taylor found him and escorted him back to the base.

Burke filed an appeal, asking the navy to reconsider the Taylor case. On November 19, 1947, the Board for Correction of Naval Records exonerated Taylor. "After careful and conscientious consideration of all the factors of the case, the board was of the opinion that the flight had disappeared for causes or reasons unknown."

Taylor was no longer blamed for the loss of Flight 19. But that didn't change the opinions of some investigators, who still claim Taylor was at fault. The controversy remains alive to this day. The missing planes have never been found, and the mystery remains unsolved.

Bruce Gernon feels closely associated with the lost pilots of Flight 19, and thinks that his experience in an electromagnetic storm in 1970 was related to what happened on that day twenty-five years earlier. "When I first heard about Flight 19 in 1971, I suspected that the squadron flew through an electromagnetic storm similar to the one I experienced."

Gernon read everything that had been written about the flight, and today, more than thirty years later, he's still convinced that he and the pilots of Flight 19 encountered the same unknown meteorological phenomenon. He points out that weather conditions tend to repeat themselves in nearly identical form. A large thunderstorm may materialize at a certain location, and the next day a very similar storm appears there at the same time of day. A large cold front may traverse North America on a particular day in the winter, and years later a similar cold front will pass through on the same day. A hurricane may travel from Africa and blast through the Caribbean, then turn north and dissipate in the Atlantic. Many years later, an identical hurricane may take the same path on the same days.

"I believe a similar cyclical phenomenon occurred on December 5, 1945, and again on December 4, 1970, at the same location over the Great Bahama Bank. Both storms were born at 3:00 PM, and they died about half an hour later. Because of the speed in which the storm appears and disappears, it isn't noticed on radar. The storm I flew through was about fifty miles in diameter, which placed its northern extremity in the path of Flight 19.

"I'm convinced that Flight 19 entered this storm at about 3:30, and exited it less than ten minutes later just before Charles Taylor made his first distress call. I suspect that Flight 19 penetrated too deeply into the storm and into a field of electromagnetic energy. By staying within the storm for close to ten minutes, they were overexposed to the electromagnetic energy, which had a dramatic effect on the outcome of their flight."

While there is no definitive proof that Flight 19 entered an electromagnetic storm, or that such a storm could affect the minds of the pilots, we know that storm conditions were present during the flight, that both of Taylor's compasses had malfunctioned, and that his thinking seemed illogical. He was confused and disoriented. When they passed over the Cross Cay Islands near Abaco, Taylor thought he recognized the Florida Keys and couldn't shake the idea, in spite of evidence to the contrary.

However, Gernon feels that Taylor can't be blamed for the disappearance of the planes. He had no record of mental aberrations and he was a distinguished navy pilot.

"If everything had been normal, it would've been a simple maneuver to head west, back to Fort Lauderdale. But everything was not normal, and all the pilots were having the same problem as Taylor. All the radio controllers who talked to Flight 19 advised them to fly west, but it seemed beyond their comprehension. None of them even used their ZBX, an instrument that would have guided them back to the base.

"I'm convinced that a lost pilot, especially a group of lost pilots, who were running low on fuel, would tend to search for the islands that they'd passed over within the past hour and a half. Flight 19 made no such effort. Instead, Taylor led the fleet of planes out to open sea in stormy weather. They headed north, then east, then west, then east again. But they never turned back to the islands, where they could've ditched safely near shore."

Instead, they flew on into oblivion, into history.

Fog That Clings

In February 1996, Bruce Gernon encountered electronic fog for a second time in a flying career that spanned three decades. As a result of that flight, he would realize an astonishing fact about the nature of electronic fog. Up to then, he had never understood how he and other pilots who have entered a similar fog could fly for miles through the murky air, while airport traffic controllers were reporting clear weather conditions with no extensive areas of fog.

On that day, Gernon and his wife, Lynn, took off from Tavernier in the upper keys, on a flight for West Palm Beach. He called Miami Flight Service for a weather briefing at about 8:00 AM. The weather in South Florida was clear, with visibility about six miles and wind out of the east at ten miles per hour. "A few medium-sized thunderstorms were starting to form over Florida Bay," he recalled. "So we had to get going before the storms reached us."

They waited patiently in their Cessna Centurion while Carl Burton, a neighbor and friend, took off in his Cessna Skymaster. Gernon didn't know it at the time, but Burton's flight would impact his own. About fifteen minutes after Burton departed, they taxied along the runway. Gernon noticed that a thunderstorm just to the west was starting to spread toward them. They needed to get in the air and away from the storm as soon as possible. Light rain from the storm pelted the windshield as they lifted off the runway and climbed over Florida Bay.

As they headed north toward the Everglades, at about 2,000 feet, they heard Carl Burton announce that he was fifteen miles to the north and he would be landing back in Tavernier. "I thought that he must have gone up for a practice flight and was returning so quickly because he wanted to land before the storm hit. I called Carl on the radio to let him know that I had just departed, so he would be aware of my position. I've talked to Carl on the radio while flying many times, and I noticed that his voice sounded tense. He always liked talking to me on the radio, but this time he seemed subdued and said very little."

Just before the Gernons reached the Everglades, another neighbor called Burton on the radio from the ground. He knew that Burton was going to Tampa and asked why he was coming back. Burton responded: "We had to turn back because the weather is just terrible! It looks like the whole state is socked in with heavy fog."

Gernon was puzzled. There were no reports of fog in the weather briefing. But he knew that fog could form quickly, especially right after sunrise. He was aware there were two known types of fog: radiation fog, which is also known as "ground fog," and advection (or "sea fog"), which forms over bodies of water. Radiation fog forms when cool ground contacts warm air, while sea fog forms when moist air moves over colder water. Unlike ground fog, sea fog can move rapidly and form at any time of day. It's usually more extensive and remains longer than radiation fog.

"It seemed we were looking at radiation fog, and it probably wouldn't burn off for several hours. I wasn't sure what to do. I only had about two hours of fuel left, and the airport in Tavernier was probably being pounded by a large thunderstorm. As we continued inland over the Everglades, all we could see was thick fog all around us, and I was starting to get tense. I was concerned that we'd run out of gas before the fog dissipated."

Gernon called Miami Flight Service for an update on weather conditions. He said he was ten miles south of Homestead, and it appeared that he was flying above fog. He asked about conditions in Miami and was told there was no fog and that the visibility was six miles. "I couldn't believe what he'd just said. I still didn't know what to do."

Gernon looked north toward Miami, but could see only a thick blanket of fog. So he asked where the fog ended. The weather briefer responded, "I have no idea what you're looking at. There's no fog anywhere in this area."

Now he was even more puzzled, and decided to fly out over the ocean in the hopes that the fog would vanish over the water. En route, Gernon studied the fog more closely and noticed something strange. There was no fog directly below the plane. As they flew on, the opening remained below the plane.

"As we headed toward the ocean, I noticed that the cylinder below us started to expand, but it remained directly below us.

I could see the earth passing below us. We couldn't get out of the fog. It seemed to be moving right along with us, at about 180 miles per hour."

It didn't make sense to him. How could there be fog all around, but none below them? He didn't know the answer. Then he noticed something else that was just as puzzling.

"As I looked through the expanding opening toward earth, I noticed a distinct line separating the fog and the ground. There was a kink in the line, which I focused on. Eventually the opening expanded all the way to the horizon, but the warped line didn't disappear as it should've done."

About four years later, after reading another case of a pilot caught in a similar weather condition, Gernon recognized the true nature of electronic fog. "That's when I finally realized that we weren't flying *through* a fog. Outlandish as it sounded, the fog was attached to the plane, therefore moving along with it. Our sense that South Florida was blanketed in fog was wrong, just as the weather briefer had told us. We had been fooled by electronic fog, and so had our neighbor Carl Burton."

Gernon tried to relax as he watched one of the most curious meteorological events he had ever witnessed. After another ten minutes, the kinked segment in the line between the fog and clear sky above started to fade and the fog began to dissipate. "Although the fog disappeared, I could see remnants of the kinked line in the distance encircling the airplane like a halo for the rest of the flight, which lasted another twenty-five minutes. The warped line even remained visible on the final approach, so that it seems possible that the fog could stay attached even upon landing."

Origin of the Name

Gernon is convinced that many pilots have flown into electronic fog without realizing it. When a pilot from New Jersey read about Gernon's 1970 experience, first recorded in *Without a Trace*, by Charles Berlitz, he called and told Gernon about a similar cloud he'd flown through on a flight between the Florida Keys and Vero Beach, Florida.

He was about five miles offshore of Fort Lauderdale on a clear day when his plane suddenly entered a fog or haze. It was like nothing he'd ever encountered. It reminded him of static on a television after the cable goes out. "He said it was like electric fog. After he hung up, I said to myself, 'No, electronic fog.' That's how I came up with the name."

Pursued by Fog

One day while having the upholstery of his single-engine Maule repaired, Gernon began talking with the upholsterer Tony Doubek about his experiences with electronic fog. To Gernon's surprise, Doubek responded with his own story about an encounter with the mysterious fog. In Doubek's case, the incident took place at sea level while he and a friend were fishing one night in 1992.

The two fishermen were five or six miles off the coast of Palm Beach County when at about 1:00 AM. they noticed glowing lights on the horizon to the northeast. The lights got brighter, then turned greenish.

"At first, we thought it might be a ship moving our way," Doubek recalled. "As it got closer to us, it appeared like a bubble of light."

When it was about a mile away, they saw that it was a luminous bank of fog. It kept coming toward them, and they were getting anxious. They started the engine when it was a couple hundred yards away. "It looked like a translucent green wall. But it wasn't wispy like regular fog. It was flat on top and rounded on the sides and was about 400–500 yards across."

To their surprise, the fog seemed to keep pace with them. "It made a beeline right toward us. I turned toward the beach, and we were moving at about 25–30 knots trying to get away from it, and it was closing in on us."

Finally, when they were about a hundred yards from shore, it began to break apart. "We didn't talk about it afterward. It was just too weird, getting chased for miles by a green bubble of fog."

Doubek doesn't know what would have happened if they'd been caught by the fog, and at the time he definitely didn't want to find out. "I was just glad to get back to land."

Dead-Air Space

Those who have survived encounters with electronic fog are the ones who can testify to its existence and who can speak for the many others who entered the fog and lost their lives. Another such survivor is a pilot named Cary Trantham, who flew into the fog in 1995 on a flight in the Florida Keys. Trantham is the manager of a flying club at the Boca Chica Key Naval Air Station, and, having flown the club's Piper Warrior many times, was familiar with the route.

On that particular day, Trantham had flown to Ormond Beach in central Florida to visit her daughter. They met at the airport, went out for lunch and shopping. On her way back to the keys, Trantham dodged scattered clouds on her flight south. The sun was low as she flew over Tampa-St. Petersburg and, as she neared Naples, she saw the lights of Miami to the east. Overhead, high clouds blocked the moon and stars. Then, as she passed over the Everglades, a haze formed below her.

"Suddenly, it was as if someone threw a blanket over the airplane," she wrote in an article published in the April 2003 issue of *AOPA Pilot*, an aeronautical journal for general aviation. The horizon was gone. She panicked. She didn't know if she was right-side up or upside down.

When she looked at the instruments, her confusion intensified. The compass was spinning. The illumination in the cockpit began to fluctuate from dim to bright and back again. "The altitude indicator began to roll, and there was a high-pitched buzzing in my headset."

She recalled a conversation with a jet pilot in the Navy flying club. He'd told her that there was dead-air space in an area over the Gulf between the mainland and the keys. She thought about a documentary she had seen about the Bermuda Triangle, with its missing planes and boats, instrument malfunctions, and magnetic anomalies. She couldn't help wondering if she was going to be the next victim.

She tried making radio contact with Miami, but there was no response. Terrified, she fought off panic. She shifted frequencies and was relieved to hear the voice of an air traffic controller. About twenty minutes later, she knew that she'd escaped the fog when she saw lights on the horizon and was told it was Marathon. She followed the string of keys and eventually landed safely back at the naval air station.

"I realized how lucky I was, and how close I came to the 'dead-man's spiral' and being another lost airplane in the Bermuda Triangle. I don't question why I survived. For whatever reason, it was a miracle, as all odds were against me."

A Classic Case

One of the best documented encounters with electronic fog occurred on June 11, 1986, when a Consolidated PBY-6A Catalina took off from Bermuda en route to Jacksonville. Aboard the Catalina were several experienced pilots: Captain Art Ward, a U.S. Navy pilot and instrument instructor, Randy Sohn, a jetliner captain for Northwest Airlines, and Major General Malcolm Ryan, a test pilot and combat leader. Also on board were the Catalina's owner Connie Edwards, his wife Karen, and author Martin Caidin and his wife Dee Dee. All four were experienced pilots. Caidin, an author of more than a hundred books, including many on aviation, later wrote about what happened on this flight.

The Catalina, which Caidin described as a large flying boat, was outfitted with state-of-the-art navigational equipment, including two location finders, a radar altimeter and multiple radios. Their navigation systems would let them know if they were so much as a tenth of a mile off the planned course. They were linked to a weather satellite, which allowed them to print out photographs taken from space showing where they were flying at that moment.

They took off for Jacksonville in clear, calm weather, expecting an uneventful flight. Caidin was standing between the two pilot seats watching dolphins through the side window when he shifted his gaze from the right side of the plane to the left. One moment he was looking out over the wing, and the next moment the wing vanished into a thick yellow cloud or fog that had risen up to 4,000 feet and engulfed the plane. "Suddenly, without a bump or a tremor or any indication that things were different, the outside world was gone," Caidin recalled. "Nothing had changed except that the airplane now was flying through a huge mass of yellow eggnog."

Abruptly, they'd entered Instrument Meteorological Conditions (IMC), but when the pilots looked at the instruments they were startled to see that all the gauges were failing. The LORAN was useless, incapable of finding anything. The needle on the magnetic compass swung back and forth, then spun in a blur. The gyroscopic instrument that created an artificial horizon failed. Even the electronic fuel gauges became erratic. "Our intricate navigation gear blinked a few times and then every dial read: 8888888. Then the radio went dead!"

In spite of the fog, they were surprised to discover that they could look through a tunnel above the plane and see a tiny patch of sky. They also could look down through the tunnel and glimpse the ocean. They continued flying in what they hoped was a westerly direction by aiming the plane toward a bright area above the horizon. The only instrument that worked was a turn-slip-skid indicator that "operated like a seal balancing a ball on its nose, and functioned without outside power."

They flew in the fog for more than three hours. During that time, they descended as low as twenty-to-thirty feet and found the fog remained with them. They went up as high as 8,000 feet and found the same "eggnog." About ninety minutes outside of Jacksonville, they suddenly emerged from the yellow sky and into bright, clear air. They looked back and there was no sign of the fog. They took a wide turn for a better view. "The sky was absolutely clear behind us as far as we could see. Whatever had enveloped us for hours was gone."

And all the electronic equipment was operating again. With the radios working, they contacted Jacksonville Naval Air Station and proceeded to land without any difficulty. They had survived an encounter with electronic fog, but only because they were experienced pilots and took turns piloting the plane.

Caidin's conclusions about the flight come close to describing the nature of electronic fog, but without using the term. "The single explanation that appears to make sense is that the Catalina flying boat was enveloped or affected by an intense electromagnetic field that dumped the instruments and 'blanked out' the electronic equipment." He added, "Any pilot caught in that 'soup' who lacked experienced flying skills with basic instruments and no outside reference would almost certainly have lost control and crashed in the ocean."

Gernon was impressed by the similarities between the Catalina flight and his own experiences in electronic fog. In his first flight his electronic equipment malfunctioned. Like Caidin, when he left the fog, it was nowhere to be seen when he looked back. In his second experience, Gernon also noticed the opening in the fog directly below the plane. It was after reading Caidin's account of the flight that Gernon came to his conclusion that electronic fog attached itself to airplanes.

It creates an illusion that it goes on and on, mile after mile. But as Gernon discovered, it's actually a localized fog that may radiate out only a quarter of a mile, and it clings to the aircraft.

PART 2

Beyond the Fog

Keeping Tabs
on the Triangle

Anyone looking for reports of mysterious happenings in the Bermuda Triangle in recent years only needs to go as far as the nearest grocery-store counter. The tabloids have kept the fire burning. While known more for invention than accuracy, the tabloids have recognized the Bermuda Triangle as a good story, one that resonates with readers.

Listen to these accounts, which were published in the *Weekly World News.* On November 6, 2001, about a month after the building housing the publication became the first target of the anthrax attack, the tabloid offered three tales from the Devil's Triangle, another moniker for the mysterious region.

One story tells of a young German girl who was born on a cruise through the Bermuda Triangle, and now possesses extraordinary psychic powers. According to a psychotherapist named Dr. Gunter Beil, five-year-old Mina can move small objects with her mind and read unspoken thoughts of people around her. The family links the child's powers to her place of birth. Supposedly, she arrived during a forty-five-minute period when everyone on board the ship felt disoriented, distracted, and apprehensive. The implication was that mysterious influences were at work at the time Mina was born. Of course, simply the fact that a baby was being born at sea might also cause those on board to feel distracted and apprehensive, if not disoriented. But the stories in the *Weekly World News* get stranger.

Spirits at Sea

Take the story of Shannon Bracy, a forty-two-year-old nurse from New Zealand who supposedly came face-to-face with the spirits of airmen and seamen wandering about in the limbo of the Devil's Triangle. On the last leg of a sailing adventure from Christchurch, New Zealand, to Bermuda, she was entering her noon position in the log when suddenly she noticed a fog settling in around her vessel. Within a couple of minutes, everything had turned stark white.

"Suddenly, I wasn't on my boat anymore. It was like I was in an eerie, desolate void. Then the spirits came. I saw men in seamen's dress and men in uniforms with wings on their flight jackets. I saw other men and women, too, even little children. They were all lifeless, drifting beings with expressions of great pain and sorrow on their faces."

She cried out for help, begging God to save her, and then she found herself back in the cockpit of her sloop. But now it was near midnight and she'd lost twelve hours. "People have told me that it was all just a terrible dream, but I don't think so," Shannon said in the story, which was first published in the Australian *World Adventures Magazine.*

The Undead Captain

Then there's the even more peculiar tale involving Captain Barney Spooner, the skipper of the trawler *Matilda II.* After Spooner apparently suffered a heart attack and died, his wife and sons decided to abide by his longstanding wish to be buried at sea. They wrapped him in a blanket, tied an anchor around the body, and threw him overboard. But, according to the account, in a feat that would make Houdini envious, Spooner turned up alive three days later. His family and the crew of the *Matilda II* spotted him floating near the vessel, and one of his sons pulled him aboard a dinghy.

"There was no doubt in our minds that Dad died," eighteen-year-old Jonathan said. "He just keeled over and that was it. He had no heartbeat, no pulse, and no breathing."

Spooner said he awakened into a mysterious, alien world. "I saw them all . . . every one of those ships and planes that had been swallowed up in the Devil's Triangle. I saw the lost ships—the *Cyclops,* the *Marine Sulphur Queen,* the *Raifuku Maru,* and *Witchcraft.* And I saw the planes—the five Navy Avengers, the Star Tiger, and so many other planes. They were everywhere . . . And I saw the faces of all the people who had vanished. They drifted past me like a slow-motion film. They had no expressions on their faces. They were just images frozen in time."

In the last two tales, we are taken into a realm in which the Bermuda Triangle becomes the equivalent of the underworld of mythology, a mournful abode of lost wandering souls, who are mere pale reflections of their former personalities. While the Gulf Stream flows through the Bermuda Triangle, Acheron, the river of affliction, and Cocytus, the river of lamentation, flow through the underworld of the Greek myths. Although scholars might dispute the analogy between an area that exists in the physical world and one associated with the ethereal dominion of mythology, the Bermuda Triangle is both real and otherworldly. The region is a place where extraordinary things happen; it's a popular urban legend, and it's an archetype, a model from our collective unconscious that has a life of its own. In a nod toward that perspective, *Weekly World News* noted that the articles on the Bermuda Triangle were published in response to requests from readers for more on the mysterious region.

The Putnam Parallelogram

One of the strangest stories related to the Bermuda Triangle appeared on the Internet in 2002. It was called the *Putnam Parallelogram: Iowa's Answer to the Bermuda Triangle?* The author is listed as Dr. Leonid Rosenweitz.

The article refers to a section of rural farmland in Fayette County near the town of Putnam that is called the Putnam Parallelogram. According to Rosenweitz, "This area occupies a disturbing and almost unbelievable place in Iowa's catalog of unexplained mysteries. More than eighty farm vehicles, cars, trucks, and small airplanes have literally vanished into thin air since 1945. More than seven hundred lives have been lost over the last twenty-six years alone, without a single body or even a piece of wreckage having been found."

Don't bother looking for Putnam, Iowa, on a map or making inquiries in Fayette County about the mysterious parallelogram. The story is a hoax and originally the basis for a play. But it took on a life of its own on the Internet, momentarily capturing the interest of more than one researcher of anomalous phenomena. The news spread to other websites, only to be later exposed like a poorly faked crop circle.

Dr. Brown's Crystal

Next comes Dr. Ray Brown and his crystal ball. He supposedly discovered a pyramid in 1970 that was not only in phenomenal condition, but was illuminated on the inside. The unlikely story has appeared several times over the years in magazines and books about Atlantis or mysteries of the unknown, and now an update on Brown and the crystal exists on the Internet, hence taking the story into the twenty-first century.

While scuba diving near the Berry Islands in the Bahamas, Brown claims that he came upon a pyramid structure with a smooth, mirror-like stone finish. Swimming inside through an open doorway, he found the interior to be completely free of coral and algae and illuminated by an unknown light source. In the center, he found a sculpture of human hands holding a four-inch crystal sphere, above which was suspended a red gem at the end of a brass rod.

Brown says he plucked the crystal from the hands and took it with him. It supposedly has mysterious powers. Both cold and warm layers of air surround it, and a breeze can be felt near it. Other witnesses have seen phantom lights, heard voices, or felt tingling sensations while looking at it.

Brown's story sounds more like a dream or a fantasy story than a reality. Only in such realms would it be possible to encounter a twelve-thousand-year-old pyramid in perfect condition below the Caribbean. Regardless, the story has taken on a life of its own.

Dr. Cornelius van Dorp says he knew Ray Brown, and when he held his crystal ball, he saw smoky pyramids inside it. In his autobiographical tale, *Search for the Feathered Serpent*, van Dorp tells of being a doctor in Antarctica and a journey through Latin America. Before he set out on that journey, van Dorp followed a trail to Brown's pyramid crystal. He discovered that Brown had died a year earlier and that now a man he called "Merlin" possessed the pyramid crystal. At first, when he meets Merlin in Cornville, Arizona, he doesn't think it's the same crystal ball. But later he recognizes the smoky pyramids again and knows that he has found the mysterious crystal.

So, if we are to believe van Dorp, a man called Merlin who lives in Cornville, Arizona, has an artifact from Atlantis by way of the Bermuda Triangle. Of course that sort of evidence won't impress scientists since the artifact is no longer in situ.

Missing Crew

Compare those stories with the following tale that surprisingly was published July 16, 1997, in the London *Times*, a newspaper not known for publishing wild or speculative tales.

In early July of that year, the British royal Navy frigate HMS *London* came across an abandoned vessel 275 miles off Bermuda. "She looked immediately strange," said HMS *London*'s commander Iain Greenlees. "She had no sails, there were mooring ropes over the side. When we got no response, we sent a team to investigate."

Officers boarded the fifty-foot German ketch, named *Ruth*, and found clothing on a bunk, an overflowing ashtray, and a book left open, as if someone had just stepped off five minutes before. But after finding rotting food in the refrigerator, they checked with authorities in Spain, and Greenlees discovered that German owners Ralf Shilling and his wife had last been seen sailing west from the Canary Islands in September 1996.

The crew cleaned up the vessel, which apparently had been adrift for ten months, and made minor repairs to the otherwise seaworthy craft. Once the repairs were complete, the Royal Navy crew headed to Puerto Rico. But before long, the Bermuda Triangle also vexed the new crew. They encountered huge storms, their navigation equipment failed as did the engine. Using sails, the crew persevered. Then, according to the *Times* article: "Once out of the Bermuda Triangle, the equipment started working again, and the crew arrived safely in Puerto Rico to rejoin the HMS *London* on July 12."

The story doesn't end there, though. Later that month, journalists found the Shillings living in Dusseldorf, Germany.

They had been visiting friends in the Canary Islands on the first leg of their journey when the ketch disappeared from a marina. Although it's possible that the boat came unmoored and drifted for ten months across the Atlantic, it's doubtful that the ketch would avoid storms and high seas that surely would have overturned the ashtray and upset other items in the cabin.

Possibly the craft had been stolen. But if that was the case, whatever became of the crew of thieves?

All Hoaxes and Lies?

So, what are we to make of these stories? Are they simply hoaxes perpetrated by writers who favor a good story over accuracy? Perhaps so, especially in the case of some of the tabloid tales. While it's easy to write off all such bizarre yarns as make-believe, Bruce Gernon, upon reading the stories in *Weekly World News*, noted that the same tabloid published an article about his experience. While no one from *Weekly World News* ever interviewed him, the story was essentially correct, the same one that he has told for three decades to everyone who would listen.

The bottom line is that in spite of hoaxes, in spite of debunkers who automatically reject all mysterious reports, on occasion things happen in the Bermuda Triangle that can't be explained. Usually the incidents occur so quickly that there is no time for a mayday call, so there is no explanation whatsoever. Planes simply fall off the radar, and ships vanish below the waves, oftentimes in good weather.

As Hans C. Graber, an oceanographer from the University of Miami, has noted: "Science can explain some things that happen in the Bermuda Triangle. But there will always remain some mystery or mysterious events that even science cannot explain."

The Electromagnetic
Attractions of UFOs

In the legend, the Bermuda Triangle is a portal for alien space-crafts arriving from who knows where. It's an underwater base, a home away from home for the crafts and their mysterious alien occupants. It's a place where a UFO might levitate a ship right off the planet or disintegrate an airplane flying too close. At the heart of most legends often lies a nugget of truth. In the case of the Bermuda Triangle, the truth could be stranger than the myth.

In January 1971, just a month after Bruce Gernon flew through a tunnel in a cloud and into the electronic fog, he encountered a mysterious craft during another flight over the Caribbean, a close encounter that nearly ended in tragedy.

It was a perfectly clear night, Gernon recalls, calm and clear, a great night for a flight. "My girlfriend never had flown at night in a small plane and decided she wanted to go with me. It was about 9:00 PM when we lifted off from Palm Beach and flew south along the Florida Gold Coast.

"I kept climbing to get a better view of all the city lights. We went all the way to 10,000 feet before leveling off and accelerating slightly to a slow cruise speed. When we were directly over Miami International Airport, we headed due east while enjoying the spectacular maze of lights below. We crossed over Miami Beach and continued east over the Atlantic Ocean as we left the city lights behind. When we were a few miles offshore, the darkness of the sea appeared as a vast black abyss."

Gernon was nearing the same area where he'd exited the tunnel vortex, when he noticed an orange light to the southeast that was about the size of a planet. It was just above the horizon and appeared to be moving slowly. Suddenly, the orange light grew larger, and they watched it in amazement. It was moving directly toward them at an incredible speed and appeared disk-shaped.

"Within ten seconds it was right in front of us and it was enormous. The disk appeared to be more than a hundred yards wide and thirty yards thick. It was bright amber and filled the entire windshield as it continued toward us. It looked metallic, about three times the size of a Boeing 747, and I thought we were going to be demolished."

Just before impact, Gernon veered sharply to the left, turning as hard as possible. "I actually thought that we had no chance of avoiding a collision since we were so close to the object."

After making the turn, he looked back expecting to see the UFO moving in a westward direction. To his surprise, it was gone—as if it had instantly vanished. Gernon concedes that it could have lifted up and soared skyward. "We were just relieved to be alive."

Shaken by the experience, they returned to Palm Beach Airport without further incident.

Sightings

Like butter on bread, UFO sightings are spread across the Bermuda Triangle saga. In his enormously popular book *The Bermuda Triangle*, Charles Berlitz wrote in 1974 that "no investigator of events in the Bermuda Triangle can avoid confronting reports of UFOs (unidentified flying objects)." One of the controversial aspects of the Triangle legend involves the question of whether the lost ships and aircraft disappeared into the depths of the Atlantic or vanished into thin air.

Berlitz and other writers of Bermuda Triangle books of that era suggest that UFOs might be responsible for many of the mysterious ship disappearances. Berlitz cited M. K. Jessup, author of *The Case for the UFOs*, who wrote that some of the famous disappearances of vessels were "almost impossible to explain except as *upward* . . . Something operating from above, with great and decisive power, and suddenness of action. . ."

As above, so below. Berlitz wrote about UFOs that were seen not only in the sky, but below the water, suggesting the idea of an underwater base in the Bermuda Triangle. Supposedly, witnesses such as Captain Dan Delmonico, who in 1973 reported two sightings of underwater UFOs, could tell that the underwater vessels weren't submarines. It all added to the intrigue and legend.

However, examining the hundreds of reports of underwater UFOs on an Internet website (www.waterufo.net), there have been none reported in the Caribbean since the 1970s. If there ever were such an underwater UFO base in the Bermuda Triangle, it may have relocated to the North Atlantic or off the coast of Italy, two areas reporting numerous sightings of underwater UFOs.

Although Gernon prefers to distance himself from those who avidly pursue the study of UFOs, or claim they've been abducted by aliens, he readily admits that he has spotted UFOs on some twenty occasions. He has seen them while he was flying, and also while his feet were planted firmly on land.

On December 30, 1974, he and his wife, Lynn, and other passengers on a commercial jet flight, watched a large amber-colored UFO for several minutes. "We were descending toward Palm Beach International and were about fifty miles north over the city of Stuart. We were at about 6,000 feet and about three miles inland when we first saw the UFO," he recalled. "I was looking east toward the ocean at 7:25 PM when a huge disk-shaped object appeared at an altitude of 3,000 feet. It was just offshore and flying south. It looked like the UFO that I'd almost collided with four years earlier. It was the same color and it seemed to glow from within, creating a metallic appearance. On the upper portion I noticed a bulge, like a cap, similar to a cockpit."

Gernon snapped several photos of the craft. At first, it was moving slower than the plane, which actually passed it. Before it disappeared from sight, he took several photos of the moving object. Although the object appears distant and somewhat hazy against the dark sky, it looks like an oval-shaped craft and the bulge at the top is clearly visible.

He noted that there were no thunderstorms in the area, and the visibility was about ten miles with patches of cumulus clouds between 2,000 and 4,000 feet. "It would disappear from sight when it passed through the clouds, but we could still see an amber glow from within the cloud."

The next night, feeling that another UFO would make an appearance, he and Lynn went to the beach and brought along binoculars with zoom lenses. This time, they saw a series of UFOs at Delray Beach. The weather was clear with no clouds, and visibility was over ten miles when they spotted the first UFO.

They watched it for about ten seconds until it vanished from sight. Just as it disappeared to the south, another appeared to the north, identical to the first one. Again, the UFO traveled at an incredible speed from north to south. Then a third UFO appeared, as if they were moving along the same flight path. It was followed by a fourth and a fifth disk-shaped object. Zooming in with the binoculars, he could see that they were identical in shape and color to the one he'd seen the previous night.

The last one flew closer to shore. It appeared to be about ten miles off the coast and traveled at the same high speed as the others. "When it was almost adjacent to us, it made a remarkable maneuver, a high-speed 90-degree turn, with no curvature in its flight path. It headed due west at an altitude of approximately 2,000 feet, and within a few seconds it passed within half a mile of us. When it reached the mainland, it flashed a blue light several times, then vanished."

In spite of nearly crashing into a UFO, and after seeing so many others, Gernon doesn't believe that they are physical vehicles from another planet. He thinks they might be an unknown atmospheric condition that could relate to electromagnetic energy. "It would be hard to believe that the UFO I nearly hit could have made such an incredibly sharp turn and have living beings inside. The G-forces in that turn would crush any living creature."

While he concedes that such a vehicle could be "unmanned" and remotely controlled, he tends to look to another explanation. "I'm not convinced that the so-called flying saucers that I've seen are controlled by aliens. People who have encountered aliens believe they did meet them, but I tend to think such experiences are related to some sort of mass mental image that we have of outer space aliens that affects the subconscious thinking of some people, so they believe their experiences actually happened. In reality, they could be having vivid dreams or waking hallucinations."

UFOs and EM

UFOs and electromagnetic energy (EM) seem to go together. One theory is that their propulsion system functions with EM and that's why those who have experienced close encounters sometimes are physically affected by the energy surrounding the vessel. But could the opposite be true? In other words, could it be that EM fields are generating the UFOs instead of the UFOs releasing electromagnetic energy?

Strange as that may sound, it's a view that is gaining increasing interest and serious consideration. Researcher Albert Budden, who has studied the effects of electromagnetic energy (EM) on humans, takes Gernon's idea even farther. He believes that UFO encounters, and even alien abduction experiences, are related to exposure to electromagnetic energy.

Although his research doesn't extend to the Bermuda Triangle phenomenon, he seems to provide an independent verification of electronic fog with his description of "electric mist." He calls the mist an unclassified atmospheric phenomenon and believes that it is created when electromagnetic energy is released above water. His theory also offers a possible explanation of UFO sightings over the Bermuda Triangle and elsewhere. In his book *Electric UFOs*, Budden states that electrical mist affects people in different ways. Those who are particularly sensitive to EM become confused and prone to hallucinations, which include sighting UFOs, and even being "abducted by aliens."

While Budden's explanation is not popular among most UFO researchers, and sounds like an updated version of the old explanation of UFOs as swamp gas or Venus, experiments by Canadian brain specialist Dr. Michael Persinger seem to support some of Budden's contentions. In more than seven hundred laboratory tests on volunteers, Persinger has established that EM fields can stimulate the temporal lobe of the brain creating an altered state of consciousness and causing "visionary experiences."

He published a paper titled, "The Tectonic Strain Theory as an Explanation for UFO Phenomena," in which he contends that around the time of an earthquake, changes in the EM field could spawn mysterious lights in the sky. An observer, especially one susceptible to EM, could easily mistake the luminous display for an alien visitor, Persinger contends.

So, applying this theory to the Bermuda Triangle, the appearance of a mysterious fog that clings to a plane, and the failure of electronic equipment, are actual events created by the release of electromagnetic energy. But EM also can cause visions and hallucinations, such as the sighting of UFOs, according to Persinger. These incidents don't happen everyday, of course, not even in the Bermuda Triangle, and the reason could be that they occur, as Persinger suggests, only when tectonic plates shift.

Tectonic plates float above the molten core of the earth, which is almost as hot as the sun. The plates shift their positions as a result of the constant flow of magma. The movement of the plates causes earthquakes and the release of electromagnetic energy. Powerful solar storms agitate the process when solar flares bombard the earth with charged particle clouds containing powerful electromagnetic fields.

It's well known that these geomagnetic disturbances caused by shifting tectonic plates and solar storms can influence electromechanical systems, such as found in the instrument panels of airplanes. Since the brain is a biological electromagnetic processor, there's plenty of reason to believe that these disturbances also affect electro-biological systems—in other words, humans and animals. Shifting magnetic fields may cause alterations in not only our moods and behavior, but also our perception. Persinger applies this concept and suggests that UFOs are hallucinations that are seen by those particularly sensitive to the energy fields.

Although there's an attraction to the concept of simplifying matters and dismissing all UFOs as hallucinations, the UFO question begs for a broader interpretation. It could be that some UFOs are hallucinations, while others are real. In the latter scenario, EM fields might facilitate the sighting of interdimensional crafts that would otherwise be invisible. A craft that is shifting between dimensions might appear to be making erratic, "impossible" moves, as well as sudden disappearances and reappearances.

That leads us to the question of time travel and its relationship to electromagnetic fields. Are incidents in the Bermuda Triangle, in which pilots perceive time warps, mental aberrations caused by EM? Or could powerful energy fields create an actual slippage in time? We'll take a closer look in the next chapter.

8
Through the
Looking Glass

The meteorologist listened carefully and nodded as the pilot described his experience flying into the heart of an enormous storm forming near Andros Island. While he seemed fascinated by the story, it all made sense to him: the failure of electronic equipment, the experience of weightlessness, his escape through the tunnel in the storm cloud, and even the mysterious fog that didn't show up on radar. He had a ready explanation for all of it.

But then, as Bruce Gernon told him what happened next, the meteorologist stopped nodding. This time he offered no meteorological interpretation.

"The remarkable thing was that we didn't come out of the storm ninety miles away from Miami, as we should have. We actually came out directly over Miami Beach. Somehow, we skipped through ninety miles of space."

The meteorologist muttered something about the possibility of misinterpreting data and shuffled some papers on his desk. It was clear Gernon had lost him. Time travel, after all, is science fiction, not an atmospheric condition. It relates to meteorology about as much as meteors.

For most people, scientists and non-scientists, the concept of time travel is just that—a concept, not a reality. Not even feasible. They point out the paradoxes: If time travel becomes scientific fact in the future, then where are the time travelers? And, if you can go back in time before your birth and kill your mother, how could you exist?

Tough questions. Possible answers: maybe the time travelers are here and we don't know it because they don't make themselves known, or we don't recognize them for what they are. Could UFOs be vessels from our future? Regarding the other paradox, science itself offers an answer. It's called the "many worlds" theory of quantum physics. The idea is that the universe continually splits and duplicates itself with slight variations, constantly creating alternate universes. When you go back in time, your appearance changes that world. It's no longer the same universe as the one you came from because in that one you didn't go back in time. So, in such a scenario, there are billions upon billions of universes all literally existing in the same space.

But resolving a paradox still doesn't mean that time travel is possible. If Gernon moved through time, how did he do it? What means propelled him ahead in time by thirty minutes?

One possible answer is that exposure to intense levels of electromagnetic energy can literally distort time. But before we delve deeper into how this might happen, let's look at the case of a pilot familiar with time shifts.

Time Warps Times Two

John R. Hawke may be the only pilot who experienced not one, but two time-warp experiences. He spent years in the Royal Air Force and had flown over all the world's oceans. He also had instructed aerobatics in the double-supersonic English Electric Lightning jet fighter. A large, lanky, athletic man, he was once the heavyweight boxing champion of the Royal Air Force.

Hawke could fly just about anything. He performed in many air shows with pilot/author Martin Caidin, and they became best of friends. Caidin wrote about Hawke's two incidents involving time distortions in *Ghosts of the Air*. Caidin is vague about dates, either because Hawke never told him when the incidents occurred, or it didn't matter to Caidin as much as the specifics about the airplanes and the details of the flights. From other references, it seems the incidents took place in the 1960s. Both pilots are now deceased, so there is no way of verifying these stories. But if Caidin ever doubted the veracity of Hawke's recollections, he gave no such indication in his comments.

The first "time skip" occurred when Hawke was flying a Riley Dove from Miami to Bermuda. At about halfway to his destination, he became enveloped in a glassy, yellow mist. He couldn't see the horizon or the ocean. It was probably similar to the electronic fog that Gernon encountered. Hawke was a skilled pilot and was confident that he could continue to fly on the proper heading to Bermuda by using his instruments to navigate. However, after flying in the mist for three hours, the estimated time to reach Bermuda, he was still in it and unable to see land or water.

Hawke forged ahead, flying on and on for another five hours until he finally broke free of the mist. He focused his eyes in the sudden sunlight and was astonished to see that Bermuda was directly in front of him. He contacted the airport tower and made a normal landing. It took him five hours longer than expected—but that wasn't all.

After landing, Hawke refueled the plane since the tanks should have been near empty after the lengthy flight. He was amazed to find out that he had landed with about a hundred gallons of gas. That was just about what he had estimated would be left in the tanks. However, he'd flown an unexpected additional five hours and the engine should have consumed all the extra gas.

In Gernon's case, he ended up with ten extra gallons of gas. While Hawke arrived five hours late, Gernon landed half an hour early. Had Gernon moved into the near future and Hawke back in time?

Hawke said he had no idea how it could be possible not to burn the fuel. "That bloody machine gave us five extra hours of flying and, according to the fuel in the tanks, which I personally checked after landing, it didn't consume a drop of fuel for all that time."

How could it be possible for Hawke to fly five hours and not burn any fuel? The only way it could happen would be if five hours passed for Hawke, but not for the airplane. Time must have distorted for him when he entered the electronic fog and, although he was inside the fog for eight hours, the airplane may have been in it for only three hours. That doesn't make sense unless you consider the possibility that Hawke may have entered a time loop. Five hours of apparent extra flying time passed, but as he exited the fog, he looped back to an earlier point where the airplane had flown only for three hours.

Gernon was in the fog for only a few minutes, but traveled an impossible distance. Hawke was in the fog for a long time, but traveled only a short distance. Time warped for Hawke in the reverse direction that it warped for Gernon—each one a different form of a space-time distortion.

A Leap Ahead

Possibly the most fascinating in-flight time warp story ever recorded was Hawke's second experience, a truly strange case. He was flying a twin-engine Piper Aztec from Fort Lauderdale to Bermuda. It was a delivery flight, and one that he considered an easy journey. "It was just a jump across some water. Nice little trip," he later recalled.

He was told to expect puffy cumulus clouds between 4,000 and 8,000 feet and, if he wanted to go higher, he'd find a convenient tall wind at 11,000 feet.

Speaking in his ubiquitous pilot patois, he described the situation. "I was on autopilot, everything as neat as a pin, and I'd crossed the drink a few hundred times already. It was like being at home. Everything was perfect until I found myself staring at the mag compass. I was staring at it all right, but I couldn't see the stupid thing."

The compass card was spinning so fast that it was a blur, and suddenly Hawke began feeling woozy. He was losing his sense of balance and his peripheral vision began to darken. "I'm accustomed to gray-outs, when high G-forces begin to dim your vision along the edges. But this time there weren't any G-forces involved, and I had that instinctive certainty that I was very likely to pass out."

Now his expertise came into play. He was already flying on autopilot, but that wasn't good enough. Instantly, he pushed his seat as far back as it would go. If he was going to pass out, he didn't want to fall on the yoke and send the plane into a tailspin. Before he could do anything else, he felt himself losing strength. He leaned back against the headrest and looked up through the windshield. All he saw was a creamy yellow fog. No clouds, no water, no horizon, no blue. The last thing he did before he lost consciousness was look at his watch. "My arm felt like lead, but I fixed the numbers in my head, and the lights went out."

He came awake fifty-nine minutes later. If the gauges were to be trusted, he was still flying northeast. Now he could see the sun and realized that the gauges were accurate. He felt drained, but otherwise okay. "I looked up and there was a lovely contrail. Just beautiful. Got on the horn right off and gave them a call. I told them I was under them, and asked where in the devil I was."

Hawke didn't believe what they told him, not at first. He was four hundred miles from where he'd been just an hour ago. His plane's maximum speed was about 180 miles an hour, but he was cruising at a much slower speed. But in that hour, he'd covered more than twice the distance that the plane could travel in that time. He turned due west and landed in Virginia.

Gernon estimates that the time-space distortion Hawke encountered in the electronic fog moved him ahead an hour and fifty-two minutes, and 220 miles too far during the hour he spent in the fog. It was impossible, of course. Yet, when a pilot is trapped in electronic fog, time can distort and the seemingly impossible can happen.

Wormholes

In *The Time Machine*, a classic by H. G. Wells, the protagonist settles into a special chair with blinking lights, spins a few dials, and instantly arrives several hundred thousand years into the future. England has long ago disappeared and is now a land inhabited by strange creatures called the Morlocks and Eloi.

In *Timeline*, a 1999 novel by Michael Crichton, several of the characters are sent back to the Middle Ages in a time machine. Time travelers are pushed through wormholes, but to survive the process, the subjects are disassembled into "quantum foam," a basic unit of matter within subatomic particles, then reassembled at their destination in time and space.

When Carl Sagan wrote his novel *Contact*, he consulted his friend Kip Thorne for technical help on the time travel. Thorne, a relativity expert at the California Institute of Technology, suggested that Sagan use a wormhole for time travel rather than a black hole. He reasoned that a wormhole would allow a time traveler to actually go somewhere, whereas a black hole is a one-way journey to nowhere. Thorne's idea not only gave Sagan's story more credibility, but led to a half dozen scientific papers on time travel.

In recent years, time travel has been gaining attention not only of novelists and mystics, but among scientists. Remarkable advances in quantum gravity are reviving the theory. Theoretical physicists now say that the theory of wormholes actually could offer a means to support time travel.

Professor John Wheeler of Princeton University created the term wormhole to describe "transit tunnels" across time and space. He describes these mini-black holes as constantly blinking in and out all around us. In other words, they exist for only a limited time.

Wormholes are like shortcuts through the universe. Mass and gravity bend space so that the universe is curved. Wormholes, which are well documented, bore through the curving or folded universe so that moving from one end of a wormhole to another is a shorter distance than following the curved surface. For example, imagine part of the universe as U-shaped. To get from the top of one side of the U to the other would require going down one side, then up the other. But a wormhole would go directly across the top of the U, a much shorter distance, resulting in a leap of space and time.

Now think of the top of either side of the U as stars. Following a wormhole through the fabric of space and time would result in a journey from one star to the other, possibly moving faster than the speed of light. If you were recording time on the journey through the wormhole, it might take six months. But when you arrived at your destination, you might find that ten years had passed. In essence, you had traveled to the future.

Wormholes are both natural—relics of the Big Bang—and artificial, created by particle accelerators. If a way were found to stabilize and expand artificial wormholes, controlled time travel would be possible. But some researchers think that nature might already be doing the trick, just as nature started fires before humans learned to control fire.

Magnetic Anomalies

A German historian, in fact, has recorded magnetic anomalies in the Caribbean. Dr. Michael Preisinger (not to be confused with Dr. Michael Persinger, the Canadian neurologist from chapter 7) spent six months in the Caribbean conducting underwater research.

Based on stories he'd heard from boaters who had experienced magnetic anomalies, such as spinning compass needles or inaccurate compass readings, he focused on six points. Three of them were near Nassau—Fish Hotel, Lyford Cay, and White Hole. The others were the Lost Blue Hole, located about an hour from Marathon in the Florida Keys, the Bimini Road near Bimini, and Sunken Train near Eluthera.

Preisinger and two other scuba divers explored each of the sites, taking readings and looking for possible reasons for the magnetic anomalies. Of the six sites, four of them consistently turned up inaccurate compass readings.

While skeptics say that inaccurate compass readings related to magnetic anomalies are not particularly mysterious, Preisinger found scientists with other ideas. In the aftermath of his study, he contacted several physicists and related the results of his underwater research. "They told me that such magnetic field anomalies could be caused by briefly appearing micro-wormholes. They could find no other explanations for the deviations."

Among them was Grazyna Fosar, a physicist from Berlin, Germany, who appeared with Preisinger in a radio interview. "From the physicist's point of view, gates to hyperspace can be the only reasonable explanation for these mysterious deviations fields."

Professor Tsung-Min Gung, a physicist from Tokyo, told Preisinger that such deviations might be a way of locating wormholes. "If the theories of interdimensional connections are not completely wrong, and can develop in the way I am expecting them to, the strong interdependencies with gravitation and the earth's magnetic field may be a way to track them down."

Time Storms

In her book *Time Storms,* Jenny Randles provided case after case of incidents of time and space distortions. Usually the circumstances involved a strange, localized fog. Sometimes it was green, sometimes yellow or white, and other times it glowed at night. What Randles calls "time storms" is similar to what Gernon refers to as "electronic fog." Also reported are electrical disorders, such as cars losing power, odd noises, gravity-defying incidents. While she has gathered cases from all over the world, most are British and on-land experiences. In some cases, time distortions took place near factories or other facilities that produced electromagnetic energy.

She cited the case of a British family called the Days, who were returning home to Aveley in Essex when they encountered a localized patch of glowing, green mist. As they entered it, their car radio started to spark as if it were about to catch fire. They felt a bump and a sensation of lifting off the road. Then, abruptly, they were closer to home and the green mist was gone. To their surprise, they had lost two hours.

Haunted by the experience and wanting to know where they'd gone for two hours, the Days underwent hypnotic regression and described an alien encounter. Randles, a founding member of the Association for Scientific Study of Anomalous Phenomena, witnessed one of the regression sessions and initially was convinced of its validity. But later she began to question the alien solution.

She noted that information obtained from hypnotic regression can be easily tainted by outside influences and, in such instances, so-called memories of alien encounters are actually fantasies. That's what Randles thinks happened in the Aveley case, which has become well known in British UFO lore. She believes that the family's alien encounter was a fantasy created under hypnosis, that the family was actually caught in a time storm—a storm in the fabric of time and space.

"The hypnosis offered an escape route from confusion and created an account of being 'beamed' into a UFO inside the mist. It was satisfying to the witnesses. It explained where they had been. It helped them to cope."

Randles, though, is convinced that the Days didn't lose two hours of memories at all. Instead they were catapulted forward in time after they entered the fog. Aliens had nothing to do with it.

The time-travel option might seem as difficult to believe as the alien scenario. However, Randles augments her arguments with example after example of supposed time-travel cases. While she admits that she was unable to document all of them, and that some might be untrue, in the end her anti-alien abduction and pro-time-travel theory is compelling and directly related to events in the Bermuda Triangle and beyond.

She speculated that time storms are a natural disturbance in the atmosphere that can disrupt time and take the form of a mini-black hole. But she acknowledges that they also might relate to years of government research involving energy fields. We'll take a closer look at that possibility in the next chapter.

Area 51 Meets the Bermuda Triangle

As the twin-engine Piper Aztec crossed the Caribbean on a June morning in 2003, Bruce Gernon looked out the side window and gazed down toward the pale blue waters of the quiet Caribbean. The Great Bahamas Bank lay 2,000 feet below. "It was right around here. This is where I saw the lenticular cloud that formed the mother storm," he said, recalling his time-travel flight three decades earlier.

Gernon was talking to a producer and crew filming a documentary on the Bermuda Triangle for the Discovery Channel as they cruised toward Andros Island, the home of a secret navy base. In the world of cable television, the Bermuda Triangle saga is very much alive and well with new productions popping up every year. Gernon was the copilot in the plane, which gave him more time to talk and look.

"Down there. Look at the water. Do you see that?" he said, excitedly. He pointed at two white patches that looked like clouds against the tranquil aqua sea. "That's the white water I told you about."

Years ago, Gernon photographed areas of white water amid the seemingly endless aqua expanses of the Caribbean. He thinks the phenomenon may have something to do with enigmatic events in the Bermuda Triangle. This time he snapped more photos as the plane made several low passes over the water. When the film was developed, the photos revealed an oblong shape that resembled an enormous white whale. In the last photo Gernon took, the white water seemed to be in the process of disintegrating.

Then they flew on toward Andros, the largest and least populated island of the Bahamas and, without a doubt, the most mysterious. Within minutes, they approached the western shore of the island and then flew over dense forest. The island's interior remains unexplored and inaccessible, a realm of the unknown. Andros, in fact, has its own mythical beings, which are said to reside under the dense forest canopy.

The chickcharnies are elfin creatures that stand about three feet tall and are monkeylike in appearance. They have piercing red eyes, three fingers, three toes, and a tail, which they use to hang from trees. Chickcharnies live in the forest and build nests by joining two pine trees together at the top. The islanders suggest carrying flowers or bright bits of cloth when touring the island in order to charm these mischievous creatures. According to legend, those who show respect to the chickcharny are blessed with good luck, while those who sneer at the creature get their heads spun around. Another creature, the lusca, is half dragon and half octopus and supposedly lives in blue holes, the island's underwater cave systems that link freshwater lakes with the ocean. The mean-spirited lusca is supposedly responsible for drowning deaths among divers exploring the holes.

After passing over thirty-five miles of forest, they reached Andros Town on the east coast, the island's main population center. Anyone expecting to find a busy commercial center is quickly disappointed. To Gernon, the town seemed frozen in time, neither growing nor shrinking over the decades. From the air, it appeared sparsely populated with residences well separated on parcels of wooded land. There is no downtown, no commercial buildings of any sort visible from the air.

But Gernon and the camera crew were more interested in another community, a secret U.S. navy base, located about a mile from the town and possibly linked to strange phenomena in the Bermuda Triangle. It's known as AUTEC, which stands for Atlantic Underwater Test and Evaluation Center. While the town has remained stagnant, the base has grown rapidly over the years, expanding like a growing suburb.

They circled low over the base after obtaining clearance from both the Nassau Tower and the Miami Air Traffic Control. "Frankly, I was surprised that we were allowed to enter the air space over the secret base," Gernon said. He attributed their success to their pilot, Stuart Hanley, a second-generation commercial airline pilot and twenty-five-year veteran of flights over the Caribbean.

No one is allowed to visit AUTEC unless sponsored by a base employee. In the early 1970s, Gernon had access to AUTEC through a good friend who worked there. So he was familiar with the base. "I noticed that they've added a huge helicopter pad large enough for a dozen military choppers to land at the same time. A Blackhawk was winding down on one pad as we passed over."

Located two hundred miles southeast of West Palm Beach, the land area of the base is only about one square mile. However, AUTEC extends out from the island to include 1,670 miles of the Caribbean and parts of the base reach a depth of 8,000 feet. According to the navy's official statement, AUTEC is an underwater range for testing and research on acoustic equipment. It includes a secret underwater submarine dock that is nearly the size of the base's land area. "AUTEC's vision is to be the Department of Defense and Navy range of choice for conducting undersea warfare testing and measurements in the Atlantic."

Then there is the unofficial version of AUTEC. Since the secret base is located in the heart of the Bermuda Triangle, it's not surprising that the base has been the source of repeated rumors and suspicions, conjecture, and dark speculation that it has something to do with strange fogs, malfunctioning electronic equipment, and even time travel. Like the Bermuda Triangle itself, a legend has formed around the secret base.

According to the legend, AUTEC is the navy's counterpart to the Air Force's super-secret Area 51, a base often associated with UFO-related activities. It conducts "black bag" projects—secret research with untraceable funding. Those projects supposedly are related to research that started with the work of radio pioneer Nikola Tesla. To that end, the legend goes, it carries on the legacy of the infamous Philadelphia experiment—a secret Navy experiment in invisibility that was said to have occurred during the 1940s and supposedly resulted in teleportation of a ship to another site, among other astonishing effects. One Bermuda Triangle website even provides details about a system that could be operating at AUTEC. It would include a VLF-resonance transmitter, a technology that might be in use by the North American Air Defense Command, or NORAD, and it would have an antipode at the center of the Bermuda Triangle. This hypothetical system would be capable of recharging secret electric-powered submarines and would definitely provide enough interference to scramble signals that airplanes and boats rely on. Hence, it would cause effects related to the Bermuda Triangle phenomena.

The Navy on the Triangle

The navy's official position on the Bermuda Triangle, which is posted on the Navy's website, sounds somewhat simplistic. The report, authored in 1974 and never updated, calls the Bermuda Triangle an imaginary area and cites bad weather as the likely culprit for the loss of ships and planes, including Flight 19. The blanket denial of the existence of any unknown phenomena at work in the Caribbean sounds oddly similar to the air force's long-standing denial of the very existence of Area 51 in Nevada.

Is the government experimenting with electromagnetic radiation and *intentionally* endangering its citizens? Probably not. However, the government apparently is conducting underwater *and* atmospheric experiments that produce EM fields, which could inadvertently create mysterious effects.

Gernon recalled an odd experience that took place near Andros Island about a year after his flight through the electronic fog. He was flying home from a trip to Providenciales with his longtime friend, Dennis Morley, and their two girlfriends when the incident occurred.

"We were cruising at 10,500 feet. It was early afternoon and we were enjoying ourselves as we watched the Bahama Islands pass by on a beautiful day. As we approached Andros from the southeast, we were flying over the deep water of the Tongue of the Ocean. I had just mentioned that we were approaching the area where I'd first entered a strange cloud a year earlier.

"When I looked over my shoulder at the two young women in the backseat, they'd both passed out. Dennis and I laughed about it. Then, just a minute later, Dennis suddenly passed out right in the midst of our conversation.

"I thought it strange that they all passed out together, just as we were approaching Andros. I couldn't understand why they were so tired. We'd all gone to bed early the night before and slept late the next day. I tried talking to Morley, but he was in a deep sleep and didn't wake up. It bothered me because he was supposed to be my copilot."

All three passengers woke up about an hour later. They had traveled about two hundred miles and were over the Gulf Stream and descending into Palm Beach. Gernon has no idea why he remained awake while the others passed out.

Did the location of the plane near AUTEC have anything to do with Gernon's initial experience or the odd behavior of his passengers a year later? It would be presumptuous and speculative to say so. Yet, there is something eerie about the fact that the last person Gernon spoke with before taking off from Andros and entering the "mother storm" was a friend, John Woolbright, who worked as a technician with AUTEC. Perhaps because of that friendship, he avoided considering the possibility that something taking place on the base was related to the storm he flew into or the electronic fog he entered after escaping the storm cloud.

"I've never wanted to believe that the government has anything to do with what happened to me," Gernon said after returning from his flight to Andros with the documentary film crew. However, he recalled that in 1973 a scientist associated with Palm Beach Community College told him that he'd most likely flown into an AUTEC experiment. "I rejected the idea. I didn't want to believe it then and I still don't want to believe it now." He paused, then added: "But over the years, it keeps coming back to AUTEC."

Electronic Warfare Simulator

While the navy's public information about the base's capabilities is limited, it does provide hints of advanced technological capabilities that sound somewhat similar to the hypothetical system mentioned above. Clearly, AUTEC has expanded its realm to the air as well as the sea with its new Electronic Warfare Simulator. According to a released document, the system "will generate complex, dynamic, electromagnetic signal environments at the radio frequency (RF) level."

The electronic warfare simulator is capable of illuminating aircrafts, surface vessels, and submarines as they move through the tracking range in the Caribbean. It consists of a radar simulator, pedestal and controller, antennas, high-power amplifiers, calibration equipment, and an operator workstation. It includes a sixty-foot tower, and the system operator is located in an instrumentation building.

There is no mention of any danger posed by energy fields to the vessels or aircrafts being tracked or to other passing airplanes and ships. But, as you'll see, similar high-tech projects involving radar in other parts of the world have purportedly produced numerous strange side effects.

Rendlesham Forest

Let's take a jaunt from the mysterious waters of the Bermuda Triangle to Great Britain, the ancient land of Merlin the Magician. In this case, the baffling magic emerged from Rendlesham Forest in Suffolk. In the 1970s, there were numerous reports of glowing green fog moving inland from the sea near the forest.

In one much-publicized incident that unfolded on December 27, 1980, three U.S. Air Force soldiers pursued a glowing light through the forest. As they moved closer to it, the air felt charged with electricity. One of the soldiers later said it seemed that hours passed as they stood watching what appeared to be a metallic, triangular-shaped craft that either hovered above the ground or rested on three-pronged landing gear. But when the glowing craft lifted up and soared away, he realized that only a few minutes had passed.

While the soldiers were chasing the glowing light, animals at a nearby farm turned frantic and electrical equipment temporarily failed. The next evening more glowing lights appeared in the sky. They made radical, seemingly impossible maneuvers, and were also seen close to the ground. Although radar detected no unusual objects in the sky, the case was interpreted as a UFO landing and has become the best known and most widely discussed case in Great Britain.

However, researcher Jenny Randles, in her book *Time Storms*, doubts that any alien crafts visited Rendlesham Forest. At the time of the incidents, an experimental physics team was working nearby on a secret project involving an advanced radar system. Randles is convinced that the mysterious effects were a side effect of those experiments.

The project in question involved over-the-horizon (OTH) radar that has the capability of picking up high-velocity missiles. OTH radar is projected into the upper atmosphere and can spot moving objects beyond the horizon. The radar ionizes the surrounding air and supposedly creates unusual and seemingly incredible side effects. Atmospheric side effects, such as glowing light, were also reported in Australia and were linked to OTH radar research.

While no definitive proof exists linking those experiments with the glowing lights and related incidents, one independent scientist has shown how he can create virtually all the enigmatic phenomena that has been reported in the Bermuda Triangle.

The Hutchison Effect

If there was ever any doubt that man-made energy fields can produce mysterious forces, the experiments of Vancouver researcher John Hutchison has put the matter to rest.

The surprising results, which have been videotaped and observed by scientists, is known as the "Hutchison Effect."

In the late 1970s, Hutchison became fascinated with the research of Nikola Tesla. He was particularly interested in Tesla's so-called "wild" ideas—free energy, levitation, invisibility, and time travel. Tesla said very little publicly about those interests, fearing that he would be scorned or ridiculed by other scientists. That concern doesn't seem to trouble Hutchison. Independent, innovative, and out of the mainstream, he pursues his interests and readily lets others know about his laboratory successes, no matter how impossible and outrageous they might seem to other scientists.

His saga began one day while conducting an experiment related to longitudinal radio wavelengths, a subject that also interested Tesla. His equipment, which included Tesla coils, RF generators, and Van de Graaff generators, was jammed into a small room in his apartment. He turned on all the devices at once and to his surprise the wavelengths that were produced combined to create something totally unexpected. As he was working, he felt a nudge against his shoulder. He turned to see a small piece of metal floating in the air.

After that, he began levitating pieces of wood, polystyrene, plastic, copper, and zinc. The objects hovered and bobbed, spun about, and sometimes shot across the room at remarkable speeds. That was just the start of the astonishing effects that manifested from more than 750 experiments. Heavy objects began levitating, including a sixty-pound cannonball. Gray fog or mists that seemed to cling to objects, similar to Gernon's electronic fog, also appeared. So did floating balls of light. A mirror shattered eighty feet from the house. Non-flammable material, such as cement and rocks, ignited outside the building. Metal warped, bent, snapped, and crumbled. Some metals became extremely hot, but didn't burn nearby pieces of wood. Water swirled in containers, driven by the mysterious force.

Even more unusual, metal objects became temporarily invisible and in one case a piece of wood merged with metal. The latter effects were portrayed in the movie *The Philadelphia Experiment*, a fictional tale based on the legendary navy experiment in invisibility that supposedly left crew members insane and some of them physically merged with the ship's deck and bulkhead. The secret experiment was based on research by Tesla, who reportedly was involved in the early stages of the so-called "Project Rainbow."

With his shoulder-length hair that sometimes falls over his face and his casual dress, Hutchison looks like the combination of an aging rock star—think Neil Young—and a "mad" scientist of the Tesla mold. In spite of eccentricities, Hutchison's work has been taken seriously by both corporations and governments. Los Alamos Lab has researched his effect, and McDonnell Douglas Aerospace and the Max Planck Institute in Germany have documented and photographed his experiments. Scientists in Japan have taken interest in his work and so has the German government.

His reception at home, however, was less than enthusiastic. On two occasions, the Canadian government seized his equipment. He was arrested and called a traitor when he tried to take his equipment to Germany. In another incident, Canadian officials ransacked his laboratory under the guise that they were searching for Hutchison's antique gun collection.

U.S. military and intelligence agencies have also expressed an interest, but Hutchison was quick to demur and remains so. A recording on Hutchison's home telephone number in the summer of 2002 welcomed the interest of movie people, but went on to say that if the caller was from the military or government, he wasn't interested. He later returned our calls and explained that he'd had bad experiences with government and military people and didn't care to deal with them any more.

Since only ordinary household electrical power of 75 watts from a 120-volt AC outlet was used to operate the machines, Hutchison believes that the astonishing effects are created by the interplay of electromagnetic energy and wavelengths among the devices. Efforts to duplicate his successes with only one of the devices operating inevitably fail.

In spite of the numerous experiments he's conducted, Hutchison still doesn't know exactly how the phenomena is created. Sometimes days go by without any positive results. Yet, his persistence has paid off and the effects were documented and photographed at McDonnell Douglas Aerospace and the Max Planck Institute in Germany.

One of the most dramatic exhibitions, which was captured on eight-millimeter film, seems to have reproduced electronic fog. On the film, objects float about the room surrounded by a gray fog, and the fog seems to cling to the objects just like the electronic fog that Gernon experienced. In another experiment, a gray metallic-appearing mist appeared that was so dense Hutchison couldn't see through it. Such a fog, if moving freely, might resemble a UFO hovering or even making erratic moves.

Hutchison also believes that these potent electromagnetic fields can form in nature as well as the laboratory. He told Gian Quasar, webmaster of the bermudatriangle.org website, that, "it's highly probable that nature can form these fields on her own and create the right situation for a ship or aircraft to either totally disintegrate or disappear and show up in another dimension."

The Bermuda Triangle might be a large-scale laboratory where electromagnetic energy released naturally from the earth or radiating from the sun as a result of solar flares produce electronic fog and other mysterious phenomena, but nature might get a helping hand from mankind in the Caribbean. Radio waves and electromagnetic energy generated at the AUTEC facility might instigate the unusual atmospheric conditions or enhance the conditions already created by nature. Hence, electronic fog and all the related phenomena.

Figure 2—The three men shortly after the flight in 1971. Layfayette, Gernon, and Gernon, Sr.

Figure 3—Gernon and the 1971 Beechcraft Bonanza that flew through the time tunnel.

Figure 4—The three men who flew through the time tunnel—Bruce Gernon, Chuck Layfayette, and Bruce Gernon, Sr., taken in 1998.

Figure 5—The birth stage of the electromagnetic storm, a lenticular-shaped cloud hovers three miles off Andros Island, as seen from the cockpit at 1,000 feet (left).

Figure 6—Trapped inside the torus-shaped squall, with no way to fly under or over, we notice the two sides of the storm meeting and forming a tunnel, and decide to fly through it (below).

Figure 7—Deep inside the tunnel vortex at 10,000 feet, wispy lines of clouds slowly rotate counterclockwise, just a few feet from the tunnel walls (right).

Figure 8—Contrails appear on the wingtips as the tunnel collapses behind the airplane. The sensation of zero-gravity results as the electronic fog captures the airplane.

Figure 9—Directly over Miami Beach, the electronic fog abruptly dissipates. The electronic and magnetic instruments simultaneously return to normal.

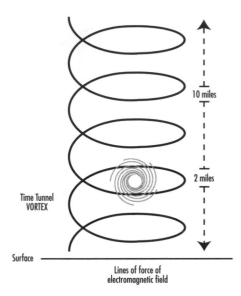

10 miles

2 miles

Time Tunnel
VORTEX

Surface

Lines of force of
electromagnetic field

Figure 10—A side-view illustration of the tunnel Gernon flew through that resulted in a time travel experience.

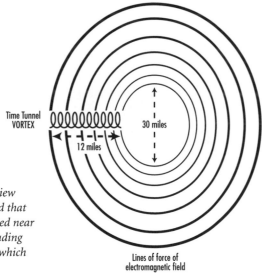

Time Tunnel
VORTEX

30 miles

12 miles

Lines of force of
electromagnetic field

Figure 11—A top-view diagram of the cloud that Bruce Gernon entered near Andros Island, including the tunnel through which he escaped.

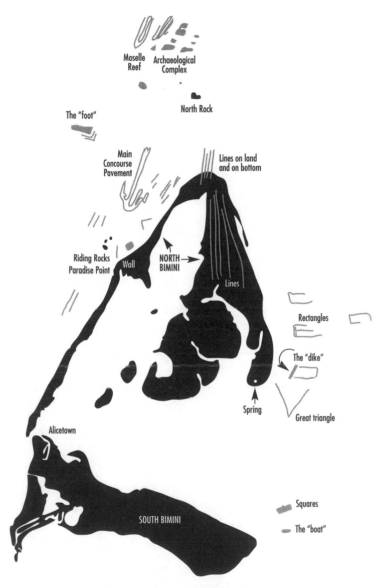

Figure 12—A map of Bimini, showing possible archaeological sites.

The Power
of Atlantis

In the story of the Bermuda Triangle, the lost continent of Atlantis looms like a subplot, an intriguing legend superimposed over the same region. An island continent as large as Europe, situated in the Atlantic, it boasted fabulous cities, advanced technology, an enlightened government, and it all disappeared in a vast cataclysm in a day and a night.

But how does Atlantis tie in with our main story? The answer is found in one word—*power*. According to the theory connecting Atlantis and the Bermuda Triangle, the energy source that powered the lost continent—and possibly destroyed it—might still be active, occasionally releasing energy fields that affect passing ships and aircraft.

The story of Atlantis was nearly lost when the Greek philosopher Plato revived it. His two dialogues, *Timaeus* and *Critias*, written about 370 B.C., were derived from two-hundred-year-old records of the Greek ruler, Solon, who heard the story from an Egyptian priest. Even at that time, the story of Atlantis dated back thousands of years.

Plato placed Atlantis in the Atlantic Ocean somewhere beyond the Straits of Gibraltar. He described Atlantis as a paradise, a land of incredible natural beauty with mountains, rivers, and lakes. The people possessed great abundance of gold, silver, brass, tin, and ivory. Their palaces were marvels of architecture and luxurious living. The Atlanteans were accomplished engineers, building a complex system of canals and bridges linking their capital city with the sea and countryside. Their magnificent docks and harbors housed fleets of vessels that carried on a thriving trade with overseas lands.

Plato described the people as gentle, wise, and virtuous. But over time they lost their noble nature and turned greedy, seeking more power and influence. In the end, the kingdom overextended itself and its warriors were defeated by the Greeks. *Timaeus* continues: "But afterwards there occurred violent earthquakes and floods; and in a single day and night of misfortune all your warlike men in a body sank into the earth, and the island of Atlantis in like manner disappeared in the depths of the sea."

Thousands of books and articles have been written about Atlantis, some claiming it as factual, others as mythical. It's as if the lost continent lives deep within the recesses of our collective memory banks. Even though no physical evidence exists to support Atlantis and scientists have dismissed the idea of a landmass vanishing in a matter of hours, the story of an advanced civilization living in a lost paradise continues to enthrall us. It simultaneously appeals to our longing for knowledge of a golden age in prehistoric times and, as a modern fable, a warning of the dangers faced by a powerful advanced civilization.

But it wasn't until the psychic Edgar Cayce (1877–1945) spoke of the lost continent as historical and located in the Caribbean that the idea of Atlantis as a close neighbor to the Americas came fully to life. Known as the "Sleeping Prophet," Cayce purportedly communicated with spirits and predicted future events. He claimed that many former Atlanteans were being born in America and that the continent would be rediscovered.

Cayce believed the Atlanteans possessed an advanced technology powered by "fire crystals." He reported from the sleeping state, in which he answered questions, that the island-continent was destroyed in a horrific disaster involving the fire crystals. Furthermore, he contended that damaged fire crystals still exist in an altered form below the Caribbean and that from time to time they release energy fields capable of sinking ships and crashing airplanes. Although the name Bermuda Triangle would not come into existence for more than two decades after his death, Cayce provided an explanation for mysterious happenings in the region. Cayce also predicted that Atlantis would begin to reappear in 1968 or 1969. Specifically, he said: "a portion of the temples may yet be discovered under the slime of ages and seawater, near what is known as Bimini, off the coast of Florida. Also, Poseida will be among the first portions of Atlantis to rise again. Expect it in '68 or '69."

No part of Atlantis has risen from the depths, with the exception of a theme park in the Bahamas by the same name. However, in September 1968, Dr. Manson Valentine, a zoologist, paleontologist, and geologist with three PhD degrees from Yale, discovered the controversial "Bimini Road." A local guide named Bonefish Sam guided Valentine to a reef off the coast of Bimini. When he looked down into the water, which was about ten feet deep, he saw hundreds of rocks with flat surfaces that were eight to ten feet across and arranged in regular patterns. The road, located about one thousand feet from shore, is approximately three hundred feet wide and sixteen hundred feet long.

Valentine later wrote of his discovery: "I was amazed to discern an extensive pavement of rectangles and occasionally polygonal flat stones of varying size and thickness, obviously arranged and accurately aligned to form convincing engineering courses. These stones had evidently been submerged over a long span of time for the edges of some had become rounded giving the blocks the appearance of giant loaves of bread or pillows. My personal feeling is that the whole fantastic complex represents the intelligent utilization by ancient man of material provided by nature and appropriate for the creation of some sort of ceremonial center."

In spite of his academic standing and his position as director of the Miami Museum of Science, Valentine, who died in 1994 at the age of ninety-two, was willing to explore subjects—Atlantis, the Bermuda Triangle, and UFOs—that other scientists typically avoided. When skeptics called his discovery a natural formation of beach rock, Valentine refuted their arguments. He explained that many of the stones were made of flint-hard micrite, rather than soft limestone beach rock. He also said that the stones didn't follow the curving beach line, that some of the largest stones are propped up at the corners by pillar stones.

From Atlantis to the Triangle

Bruce Gernon first learned of Valentine's interests on a south Florida news program in early 1974 when he appeared as the leader of a group who was conducting research on the Bermuda Triangle. Gernon called the Miami Museum of Science and left a message for Valentine, who contacted him a week later and arranged for a meeting.

Gernon remembers Valentine as a tall, handsome man in his seventies when they met. He recalls Valentine telling him about his explorations with pilot Jim Richardson, flying over the Bahama Bank near Andros Island. "They had discovered a set of perfectly straight white lines heading toward the west. They followed the lines with their airplane for almost twenty miles. The lines led them to a huge trident-shaped object that looked as if it were man-made. The trident appeared to be over one hundred feet long and at the base were three polygonal holes. They were very excited about the discovery and marked the spot so they could return to dive over the site."

Later, diving over the holes they were amazed to find the main cavity blocked by large stones. Dr. Valentine said that it was as if there had been a large explosion over the trident that had taken place after they had discovered it. Fortunately, Valentine had taken photos of the trident on his first flight over it and one of those photos appeared with a lengthy article he wrote called, "Underwater Archaeology in the Bahamas," for the *Explorers Journal* in 1976.

He began that article with this premise: *If the great, submerged plateaus of the Bahamas were dry land in the relatively recent past, as seems certain, then their shallow waters might well yield signs of occupancy by ancient man.* With that theory in mind, Valentine set off on his exploration of the Caribbean that spanned more than two decades. Although he never claimed that the Bimini underwater complex was part of Atlantis, he was intrigued by the myth of a lost continent that disappeared twelve-thousand years ago and the geological history of a landmass that disappeared into the sea at about the same time.

Gernon also recalls that Valentine was confident that the skeptics, who called the formation beach rock, were wrong. To make his point, he gave a demonstration using a one-inch thick slice of a stone cut from the site. "He held it up and then hit it with a hammer. It made a ringing sound. You can't do that with beach rock."

Valentine's research in the Caribbean encompassed both the search for Atlantis and the mystery of the Bermuda Triangle. In fact, Charles Berlitz made extensive use of Valentine's research for both of his books on the Bermuda Triangle. Valentine was fascinated by Gernon's recollection of his flight through the huge storm in 1970 and later introduced him to Berlitz. But when Gernon first related his story to Valentine, he was puzzled by the scientist's immediate reaction.

They met at Valentine's house in downtown Miami, a well-kept older home that belonged to another era of Miami and was virtually surrounded by high-rise buildings. At first, they conducted a normal conversation at a table with Valentine asking Gernon several questions about the weather conditions and situation leading up to his flight. But when Gernon started describing the flight itself, Valentine's behavior shifted.

"When I got to the point where I told Dr. Valentine that the airplane lifted off from the runway at Andros Town at 3:00 PM, I noticed that his eyes started closing. As I continued to explain the details of the flight, his eyes continued to close and he slowly lowered his head until it rested on his forearms on the tabletop.

"This startled me as I thought that he might be having a stroke or something else was wrong. I turned to Mrs. Valentine, who told me in a quiet voice that I shouldn't worry. She said that he was going into a trance and that he could still hear me. It felt strange telling my story to someone who appeared asleep, but I later came to understand that the reason he was in a trance-like state was so that he could attain a higher level of concentration to analyze my flight. I had the feeling that he was visualizing the same images that I was seeing in my mind as I spoke.

"I continued to talk for close to thirty minutes and he never moved a muscle. It was as if he'd fallen into a very deep sleep. When I finished, Dr. Valentine slowly raised his head, then opened his eyes. He looked at me, smiled, and turned to his wife Anna: 'This is amazing. He is the only pilot to have ever flown through the heart of the storm, from its birth through its maturity and to exit through the vortex.'"

Valentine thought there was a connection between the Bermuda Triangle and Atlantis. The link, he believed, was UFOs, which might be the machines of time travelers moving through portals in the Bermuda Triangle between Atlantis and other worlds or other dimensions.

Surveying the Site

Others followed in Valentine's wake, exploring the mysterious underwater complex near Bimini. Dimitri Rebikoff, a French engineer and a pioneer of underwater photography, conducted both underwater and aerial photography at the site. From 1969 to 1978, Rebikoff carried out a photographic survey of the entire site, stone by stone.

In 1974, Dr. David Zink, a prehistorian and explorer, studied the site, making professional surveys using sonar equipment and nuclear activation analysis. He used U.S. Navy divers as well as psychics in conjunction with standard archaeological procedures. He authored *The Ancient Stones Speak* and *The Stones of Atlantis*. Zink concluded that the stone complex was built by humans in ancient times.

Manson Valentine didn't like the underwater stone structure referred to as the Bimini Road. He didn't think it was a road, a wall, or even an ancient seaport. If anything, he thought it might be a sacred ceremonial center, comparable to Stonehenge or the Nazca Lines. "Such majestic artifacts are incomprehensible to us—unless, of course, we have the temerity to consider extraterrestrial interventions and metaphysically generated energies."

In spite of the research and the arguments presented by Valentine and others who have explored the stone complex off Bimini, mainstream scientists remain steadfast in the notion that the stones are a natural formation. Meanwhile, more discoveries of stone complexes below the Caribbean are coming to light.

New Discoveries

In December 2002, researchers with a Canadian exploration team confirmed the discovery of stone structures in deep water off the coast of Cuba that may have been built by a human civilization thousands of years ago. The mysterious structures look like the layout of an urban center. Paulina Zelitsky, of British Columbia-based Advanced Digital Communications, said that the stone structures could have been part of a civilization that was lost in a great geological upheaval.

The company made the initial discovery in July 2000 while using sophisticated side-scan sonar equipment. They found a large underwater plateau dotted with orderly stone structures that were partially covered with sand and located twenty-one-hundred feet below the surface. From above, it was reported that the site looked like a complex of pyramids, roads, and buildings.

The research team, along with their Cuban partners from the Cuban Academy of Sciences, returned two years later for further investigation. This time they lowered a remotely operated vehicle that filmed parts of the 7.7 square-mile complex. The images revealed huge, smooth, granite-like blocks in perpendicular and circular formations, some shaped like pyramids. Many of the blocks were between five and fifteen feet in length and some were stacked on top of each other.

Zelitsky said the discovery provided supportive evidence that Cuba was once linked to the Yucatan peninsula by a bridge of land. If the submerged structures represent the ruins of a civilization, it would have existed at least six-thousand years ago, she said. The sea level at the height of the ice age, about twenty-thousand years ago, was more than four-hundred feet lower than it is today, according to geologists, and slowly rose over the millenia. That means that the civilization would have been destroyed by a cataclysmic event, earthquakes, or volcanic activity, in order for it to sink to its current location. Such an event has happened in recorded time. In 1992, two-thirds of the town of Port Royal, Jamaica, collapsed into Kingston Harbor during an earthquake. The old town now rests forty feet below the surface of the ocean.

The Andros Site

Near the north coast of Andros Island, researchers have discovered a three-tiered stone platform lying beneath ten feet of water. Drs. Greg and Lora Little discovered the site in a serendipitous fashion. They began a series of research expeditions in February 2003 in an attempt to solve a thirty-five-year-old mystery involving underwater stone formations. In the late 1960s, while Manson Valentine was working near Bimini, pilots photographed strange, circular formations off the western coast of Andros, many of which looked like stone rings. However, as far as the Littles knew, no one had investigated the formations, which are located in a remote side of the sparsely populated island.

The couple, who are affiliated with the Association for Research and Enlightenment in Virginia Beach, Virginia, located the stone rings from the air, then investigated the sites. They were disappointed to find that all the formations had natural explanations. However, on their last night on the island, they met Dino Keller, an experienced diver and former dive boat operator, who told the Littles about an unusual stone structure he had viewed from a boat just after Hurricane Andrew passed the island in 1992. Keller told them that it looked like the Bimini Road, only larger.

The next day they found the strange formation about five hundred yards offshore. The three stone tiers are about fifty feet wide and rise about two feet above the level below. The bottom tier is formed by well preserved two-foot-thick rectangular blocks that are mostly thirty by twenty-five feet and lay side by side. The second and third tiers are formed by similar large stones.

After inspecting the site, the Littles made plans for a more detailed study and returned in April 2003, spending three days surveying and photographing the site.

The platform below the three tiers is about one-hundred, fifty feet wide and at least four hundred yards long. Geologists have suggested that the structure is beach stone and could be at least six thousand years old. But the tiers rise away from the beach, which is not what is usually found with beach rock formations. The Littles, who are cautious investigators, say the structure looks manmade, but they say they're not yet sure of it.

As with the Bimini Road, mainstream scientists are doubtful that the stone formation near Cuba and Andros Island are man-made. They want to know where the artifacts are that help define a culture. So far, none have been found in association with the stone structures. There are no ancient tools or broken pottery or bones that are usually found with ruins. However, considering the location of the ruins below the Caribbean and the storms that quickly bury and disperse wrecked ships and their cargo, it's not hard to imagine that the vestiges of a twelve-thousand-year-old civilization would be deeply buried and scattered, if not totally destroyed. Certainly, any bones at the site would have disintegrated long ago and broken pottery would be sand.

Atlantean artifacts, it seems, remain as elusive as the chickcharnies of Andros Island, or the location of a time tunnel, or the materialization of a wall of electronic fog. While the nature of the fog, like the location of Altantis, remains mysterious, the effects the fog produces among those who have been captured by it are more readily apparent. We'll take a closer look at such effects in the next chapter.

PART 3

Seeing the Fog

Short-Term Reactions

Whether its source is man-made or natural, electronic fog is real. As we contend, it not only can knock out electromagnetic equipment, but it can cause breaches in the space-time continuum. Electronic fog also can cloud the minds of those trapped within its boundaries. It causes confusion and disorientation at the time of the incident or shortly after it. People who are normally mentally sharp forget to follow basic procedures. Many pilots, caught in the fog, tailspin to their deaths.

After Bruce Gernon flew into electronic fog in his first experience in 1970, he contacted the Miami radio controller and asked for his location. To his surprise, the controller couldn't find them on the radar. "Then my dad did a highly unusual thing. He grabbed the microphone from me and began screaming and swearing at the controller. In the five years that I'd been flying with him, I'd never seen my dad act that way. He almost went into a state of panic, but I eventually got him to calm down."

But Gernon's father wasn't the only one acting oddly. "As we penetrated deeper into the fog, our passenger, Chuck, became almost incoherent. I can remember telling myself that there was no use in talking to Chuck anymore because he looked out of it. We were definitely feeling sensations that we'd never experienced."

It might seem logical that even an experienced pilot trapped in fog, in some cases, might become disoriented and his passengers might start to panic. But if you add to the equation a spinning compass and the effects of electromagnetic radiation, the chances of confusion and disorientation multiply.

That very well could have been the case with the "Lost Patrol." In spite of the extensive flying experience of the lead pilot for Flight 19, he and the other pilots were confused and disoriented and unable to find their way home. Yet, all five Avengers were equipped with ZBX, a homing device similar to today's automatic direction finder. It would be standard procedure to turn on the ZBX in order to attain a heading back to Fort Lauderdale. From the transmission that was picked up, none of them seemed to know which way was home.

Animals and Magnetism

But can electromagnetic energy really affect a pilot's decision-making abilities? Experiments with animals suggest that magnetism can do just that. It's known that some animals, including migrating birds, use the earth's magnetism to navigate. Whales are known to have magnetite stored in bundles of nerve cells that become internal magnetic field detectors that help them navigate the seas.

Pigeons have inner magnetic sensors they navigate by, even in bad weather or at night. Experiments have shown that if small magnets are placed on the pigeon in reverse order, the birds become mentally disoriented and confused and lose their ability to find their way home. Experiments also have shown that magnetism can confuse bees. When worker bees return to their hive with news about the location of nectar, they communicate to other bees by performing a complicated series of maneuvers. However, when a magnetic field is placed around the honeycomb, the dance becomes a senseless series of patterns that communicate nothing to the other bees.

Pilots and EM

When an airplane enters an electromagnetic field, how it affects the pilot and passengers varies from person to person. John Hawke passed out for an hour after flying into a strange fog. He was fortunate to survive. In 1971, Gernon's three passengers passed out on a flight near Andros Island, as they flew near the AUTEC base and the area where Gernon had encountered a strange cloud a year earlier.

Casey Purvis, who worked regularly as a volunteer pilot with the Coast Guard Auxiliary, quickly became disoriented when he flew into a localized fog off the coast of Marathon, Florida (see chapter 3). In spite of his extensive flying experience and orders from a coast guard pilot to fly north, Purvis reacted in a confused manner. He made several turns in the two minutes after he reported the fog. But he never turned north.

Purvis no doubt suffered from spatial disorientation when he lost sight of the horizon in the fog. That was the National Transportation Safety Board conclusion. But from the description of the incident, Gernon believes that Purvis encountered electronic fog and the electromagnetic energy contributed to his disorientation. "EM affects individuals in different ways. It could've caused or contributed to his disorientation, and led him into the series of turns and ultimately into a death spiral," he said after studying the report.

Cary Trantham of Key West also became confused and disoriented when she flew into a fog near sunset and her instruments malfunctioned on a flight to the Boca Chica Key Naval Air Station. She fought off panic and found her way out of the fog and landed safely.

Later, she called her survival a miracle. "I realized how lucky I was, and how close I came to the 'dead-man's spiral' and being another lost airplane in the Bermuda Triangle. I don't question why I survived. For whatever reason, it was a miracle, as all odds were against me."

Emergency Procedures

There are several reasons Bruce Gernon is telling his story about the Bermuda Triangle that began more than three decades ago. First, he wants to shed more light on the unknown atmospheric condition that he calls electronic fog and its relationship with energy fields. He hopes to bring the phenomenon closer to becoming a recognized geo-meteorological condition, one far more subtle than a hurricane, but one that can be just as deadly. To that end, he hopes his efforts encourage new scientific research. But for the present, he wants to warn pilots about the fog and prepare them in the event of an encounter with electronic fog.

Here are some suggestions he offers:

- Remain calm, don't panic. The airplane will continue flying.

- Use all available radio navigation systems and ask air traffic control for assistance.

- If the magnetic compass is spinning, other navigational equipment cannot be trusted. The sun will be located where the fog appears brightest. Use this reference as a guide to maintain your desired course. Your barometric pressure instruments will remain accurate.

- Given the circumstances and your position, you will have to decide the best course of action. Continuing with your original plans might not be in your best interest.

- If you are over water, try to fly to the mainland or the nearest large body of land. Electronic fog should detach with the temperature change.

- Likewise, if you are over land, try to fly to the ocean or a large body of water, if it's feasible. Again, electronic fog should detach with the temperature change.

- Once established on your course, avoid making turns. It will cause confusion and add to your disorientation.

- Descend to a lower altitude if land is nearby, but remain above the minimum altitude for safe clearance of obstructions such as radio towers.

- Plan an emergency landing if your fuel level becomes a factor. If land is located, plan a precautionary landing. If you can't find an airport, look for a road or field to land on.

- Autopilot may be used to maintain altitude and keep the wings level if the gyroscopic instruments are still working. Do not use autopilot to maintain a heading.

- When VFRs (Visual Flight Rules) turn to IMCs (Instrument Meteorological Conditions) and you transfer to IFRs (Instrument Flight Rules), the TC (turn coordinator) and AI (attitude indicator) may indicate a bank, but the HI (heading indicator) is indicating a straight flight because the pilot is following it. In reality, the HI and magnetic compass may be slowly spinning. In such a situation, use your imagination to maintain a heading and do not use HI or a magnetic compass. The slip/skid indicator may be the only instrument that continues to work.

Electronic Fog Basics

What is it?

An unknown geo-meteorological phenomenon that appears as a patch of fog extending no more than a quarter of a mile in any direction. It has been reported as grayish-white, yellow, and green. Sometimes it appears to glow at night.

What does it do?

It disrupts electromagnetic equipment, clings to airplanes and ships, and can travel with the crafts and vessels for hundreds of miles, giving the illusion of being vast. It can induce spatial disorientation among pilots. Its most dramatic attribute: It causes rifts in the time-space continuum, i.e., time warps, time slips, or time distortions.

How is it created?

Electronic fog is created when electromagnetic energy fields from the earth mix with water and the atmosphere. It is dispersed from a storm similar in size to a squall, except it is circular in shape and short-lived. This could be called the "mother storm" or a "time storm." EM fields might also produce visions and hallucinations, including the sighting of UFOs.

Why does it happen in the Bermuda Triangle?

Danish scientists have discovered the magnetic field is weakening more rapidly in the Bermuda Triangle than anywhere else on Earth. They speculate that the magnetic changes could result from violent turbulence deep in the molten iron core directly under the Bermuda Triangle.

EM could be released by movement of tectonic plates below the Atlantic. It also could be produced through secret government experiments. Another theory relates the release of energy to an ancient energy source buried below the Caribbean, and associated with the mythical continent of Atlantis.

Those, like Gernon, who survived to tell about it, never forget about their experience in the fog. In fact, their lives changed as a result of it. To outside observers, they might seem somewhat obsessed with the need to tell others about this enigmatic atmospheric condition and its far-reaching effects. Even Charles Lindbergh, after years of avoiding the matter, ultimately wrote about his baffling experience in the mysterious fog.

Some survivors, like Gernon and Martin Caidin, apparently gained unusual mental abilities that may be directly related to their time in the electronic fog. We'll take a look at the psychic factor in the next chapter.

Long-Term Effects

Bruce Gernon pushed his four-passenger green and white Maule from the hangar adjacent to his house at the Aero Club in Wellington, Florida, a village on the edge of the Everglades in Palm Beach County. He started the plane's engine on the concrete pad in front of the hangar and went through the checklist he follows every time he prepares for a flight. A few minutes later, the sandy-haired pilot taxied along the grass landing strip near his home and took off, en route to Fort Lauderdale. He would fly into the former navy base near the International Airport, the very base from which the infamous Flight 19 departed in 1945 and flew into eternity. But on this visit, Gernon wasn't attending a Flight 19 memorial. He was here to meet a man traveling from Miami with a story about fog and electromagnetic energy and time travel, a man whose life has been altered by his encounter with something very strange.

Ivan Lima, a handsome man in his late thirties and originally from Brazil, is an electrical engineer with a PhD. in the field. He's knowledgeable about electromagnetism, and works in the biomedical field. Like Gernon, he had an experience with fog on the ocean that he has never forgotten. Something happened that he cannot explain and he wants answers. To say that he is obsessed with the subject would be an understatement. He's intent on finding the fog again, even if it means endangering his life. He wants to learn everything he can about it. To that end, he created the Gate Phenomenon Project and is assembling electronic equipment, which he plans to install on a research vessel.

After meeting Gernon at the restaurant that overlooks a runway on the former base, they ordered lunch and Lima began his story. The incident he described occurred far from the Bermuda Triangle, yet there are some intriguing similarities between Lima's encounter with fog and Gernon's passage through it.

On October 8, 1995, Lima joined a group of medical professionals for a day of sailing and fishing on a sailboat in the San Francisco Bay area. They left the dock at 8:15 AM on a perfect day for sailing, with clear skies and quiet seas.

At about 9:30, they anchored the craft and prepared their fishing gear. Within minutes, Lima and the others noticed the air shimmering above the water about fifty feet from the ship. It looked like a mirage, created by solar radiation, as seen on roadways on a hot day. But solar radiation doesn't occur above water, or such a short distance away, or in the morning hours.

Everyone seemed mesmerized by the sight, and as they peered at the manifestation, a fog began to materialize, taking the place of the mirage. It was low, thick, and rectangular-shaped, the top of it not more than three feet above the surface. Everyone on board stared in fascination at the strange bed of fog as it moved slowly toward the boat. As they watched, the fog at the edge nearest the boat began to rise like a curtain. At the same time, it expanded laterally until it was about one hundred feet wide and seventy feet high.

No one on board moved or talked. Everyone seemed entranced. The fog continued rising until it was as high as it was wide. The bed vanished and all that remained was a vertical wall of fog, as if the fog had stood up. At first, it appeared nearly square. But after a few minutes, the wall became oval-shaped and began to rotate clockwise. There was no wind, no sound, but the bright sunny day had turned dusk-like. As the fog rotated, the center spiraled inward, forming a revolving tunnel.

The fog kept coming closer and closer, threatening to swallow the sailboat. Hurriedly, they pulled up the anchor, started the engine, and fled. As soon as they left, the clear blue sky and sunshine returned. Everyone agreed that what they'd seen could have been a gate to another dimension or another time.

"I wonder what would've happened if we'd gone into it?" Lima asked. But no one responded.

By the time they returned to the marina where they'd rented the sailboat, they were all nauseous and confused as if they'd just awakened from a trance. They were astonished that it was already 3:00 PM. Somehow, four hours had disappeared. They'd sailed directly back to the marina after anchoring for about twenty minutes at the site of the fog. Where did the time go? No one knew the answer.

Lima became more and more intrigued by what he'd witnessed. He knew he'd seen and experienced something that couldn't be explained as any known weather phenomenon.

He couldn't stop thinking about it. He read everything he could find about mysteries of the sea, and he began studying quantum physics looking for an explanation. However, when he talked to the others who had been on the boat, they didn't want to talk about the fog. They told him to forget about it. That he would never do.

Lima finished his story as lunch arrived. Gernon asked about the four lost hours. Even though the boat didn't get swallowed by the fog, the passengers were affected by it. Maybe they didn't lose track of four hours. Maybe instead they leaped ahead in time, as Gernon had done. The gate or tunnel might have been a wormhole, a passage through time. Lima agreed that the time factor was key.

But he isn't content to leave it at that. In spite of the years that have passed, Ivan Lima feels compelled to go back and find the fog. He wants to measure it, analyze it, and understand it. He's ready to enter the fog.

While he and Gernon share a fascination with enigmatic fog, Gernon is cautious. As a pilot, he thinks it's best to avoid electronic fog at all costs. He knows that he's lucky to have survived his experience. Because his life was spared, he feels that he must help others understand what's out there. He recognizes the inherent danger in any attempt to penetrate it. Lima, on the other hand, hopes for another opportunity to experience the fog, and this time he's intent on passing through the gate.

As they left the restaurant, they stopped by the Flight 19 Memorial on the grounds of the former naval air station and looked at the list of names of the lost airmen.

"One way or another, I'm still going to find that fog," Lima said. "I don't care how long it takes."

Gernon nodded. He understood Lima's obsession, if not his willingness to dive into the fog.

Rainbows and Visions

One day in early June 2003, Gernon drove his white Expedition onto the Florida Turnpike and headed south en route to Perry Airport in Hollywood, Florida, about forty miles from his home. He would be meeting a film crew making a documentary for the Discovery Channel and they would fly to Andros Island. It would be the seventh documentary on the Bermuda Triangle in which he would appear, but the first one that would take him back to Andros Island.

He was excited about the trip and looking forward to it. As he glanced out the window, he noticed a rainbow. He drove and soon spotted another one, then another and another. By the time he reached the Hollywood exit, he'd seen five rainbows. For Gernon, that was confirmation that something interesting was going to take place. And it did. His trip, described in chapter 9, included the discovery of large patches of white water, which were first described in Charles Berlitz's *The Bermuda Triangle*, and surprisingly, they were allowed to fly low over AUTEC, a secret navy base.

Gernon seems to have an affinity for rainbows. In his early twenties, he used to fly with his father from West Palm International to Pahokee, a town on the east shore of Lake Okeechobee, where he and his father were building a subdivision. On the forty-mile flight, which passed over large sugar cane farms created out of the Florida Everglades, they'd often fly near small cumulonimbus thunderstorms, which were easy to circumnavigate. During those flights, he'd seen numerous rainbows, and many times, if he could fly close enough, he would be able to look down and see the rainbow turn into a perfect circle at a lower altitude.

It was a beautiful sight, but nothing out of the ordinary. Then one day, just a week before his time travel flight out of Andros Island, he encountered a rainbow that he will never forget. It was at the end of the day and he and his father were coming back from Pahokee after work. There were many small showers in the area, and he saw a flurry of rainbows, at least twelve of them, one after another, and several of them were circular. At one point, he thought he saw four at the same time.

Then something even more remarkable happened. "As we approached a rainbow that was directly in front of our flight path, the airplane seemed to penetrate the rainbow. It looked as if we were flying through a giant ring of beautiful surrealistic colors. The rainbow appeared circular, but this time the circle was vertical instead of horizontal. The kaleidoscope of colors completely encircled the airplane in all directions as we penetrated the rings."

Skip ahead thirty-three years. At the University of Miami, Gernon and the film crew from the Discovery Channel met with Dr. Thomas Curtright, a theoretical quantum physicist, and Gernon related his rainbow story as a preface to recounting his time travel experience. Curtright listened closely, then shook his head. First of all, he said, it is impossible to see more than one rainbow at a time, as Gernon suggested he'd done.

It was equally impossible to fly through a rainbow, Curtright asserted.

Gernon conceded that he might not have seen more than one rainbow at once. He'd made no effort to memorize the experience. However, he was positive that he and his father flew into a rainbow, passing through the spectrum of colors that filled the cabin.

Curtright, who sat at a desk buried in stacks of papers, mulled over the matter in silence for a minute after hearing Gernon's confident response. Finally, he looked up and met Gernon's gaze. "You cannot go through a rainbow and see the colors, not unless you are the source of energy creating the rainbow."

Gernon later laughed as he recalled the comment. Then he added that it wasn't the first time that he'd heard such an idea. After writing an article about his experience in the "mother storm" and the electronic fog for *Fate* magazine, a journal dealing with paranormal mysteries and experiences, an editor told him that he was the source of the mother storm. "I didn't understand what he meant, and now a physicist tells me that if I went through a rainbow, I was the source of it."

One writer has suggested that people who experience phenomena in the Bermuda Triangle do so because they are more susceptible to those experiences than others. However, in Gernon's case, it seems that rather than being particularly susceptible, the opposite might be true. While he seems to attract the enigmatic experiences, just as lightning is drawn to the tallest object in its path, he also seems *insusceptible* to the forces present in the Bermuda Triangle, and that's why he is alive today.

While his passengers were confused and disoriented when they were caught in the enormous mother storm, Gernon remained calm and maneuvered the plane through the tunnel vortex, then through the electronic fog to safety. A year later, when his three passengers passed out on a flight near Andros Island, close to the area where he'd encountered that storm, Gernon remained alert and in control of the plane. Had he reacted in the same way as the others, the plane would've crashed into the sea and Gernon and his passengers would've joined the list of people lost in the Bermuda Triangle.

Gernon doesn't know why he was unaffected by whatever caused the others to pass out. He doesn't know whether he is susceptible or insusceptible to the forces that manifest from time to time in the Caribbean. What is clear is that in the aftermath of his initial experience, he developed an unusual talent, an ability to glimpse things on occasion before they happen. His precognitive experiences often relate to mysterious phenomena in or around the Bermuda Triangle.

Gernon recalls his first vivid precognitive vision three years after his experience in the fog. He was watching a television news program when a report about the Bermuda Triangle appeared. It featured a tall, elderly man named Dr. J. Manson Valentine, Captain James G. Richardson, a former navy pilot, and a world champion breath-holding diver, Jacques Mayol.

"As Dr. Valentine started talking, the television screen disappeared and I saw another image. My eyes were open and I suddenly felt very excited. It was extraordinary, because I saw Dr. Valentine and myself and both our wives dining together at a waterfront restaurant and we seemed to be friends."

As a result of the vision, Gernon contacted Valentine. They later met, as described in chapter 10, and after their meeting at the researcher's house, Valentine and his wife Anna took Gernon and his wife Lynn to dinner at a waterfront restaurant—the same one Gernon had seen in his vision.

In two other precognitive incidents, Gernon actually predicted UFO sightings. The reason he was able to photograph a UFO through the window of a commercial jetliner in December 1974 was because he predicted one would appear during the flight (see chapter 7). Likewise, he predicted that he and Lynn would see a UFO at the beach at 8:00 PM the next evening. Instead of one, they saw five, the first one appearing at 8:05.

A few months later, another precognitive impression came to him while he was talking with an old friend named Timothy Bogle. He was telling him about the mystery of the Bermuda Triangle and his own strange experiences there. Bogle, an accomplished sea captain, seemed to doubt that Gernon had ever seen anything unusual because he'd been sailing in the Caribbean for many years and never had experienced anything out of the ordinary.

While Bogle was talking about plans for a cruising party on his sailboat during the upcoming weekend, Gernon suddenly felt excited and he knew that they would see something unusual during their trip. "I interrupted him and said, 'This Saturday night, when we go out on your boat, you and everyone else will see an unusual light in the direction of Bimini.'"

Bogle laughed and neither one mentioned it again until the night of the cruise. About a dozen people gathered on board the sailboat that Saturday afternoon and headed down the Intracoastal to the inlet at Boca Raton, then out into the ocean. They sailed a few miles offshore to the edge of the Gulf Stream and headed north toward Palm Beach on a beautiful tropical Florida night.

"I had almost forgotten about the prediction when someone yelled out that they saw a strange light over the ocean in the direction of Bimini. It was not like the many UFOs I've seen. It looked more like a beam of white light being projected for several miles from about 3,000 feet above the sea."

The beam appeared to be about ten miles away and was slowly rotating clockwise. As they watched, it made three complete revolutions, each one taking about two minutes before the light disappeared. There were scattered cumulus clouds in the area and when the beam hit the clouds it illuminated them and cut off the rest of the beam. Gernon asked Bogle if it could be the Great Isaac lighthouse, but he said it would be impossible to see it because it was fifty miles away.

"I suggested that it was some sort of atmospheric reflection of the lighthouse beam that we were seeing, but he rejected that idea. He said he'd seen the lighthouse beam many times at night so he knew what it looked like. He said it was the strangest light he'd ever seen in all his years of sailing and that he had no idea what it could've been."

After that experience, Gernon's friend changed his mind about the Bermuda Triangle. "Whenever the subject came up and he was around, I used to enjoy teasing him by saying, 'Tim saw the light!'" He would always agree and say, 'Gernon showed me the light.'"

Squaring the Triangle

Gernon's strongest vision of a future event came to him in 1992 while living in the Florida Keys. He was driving on the Overseas Highway, which connects the string of keys, and had just reached the apex of one of three bridges connecting Upper Matecumbe and Lower Matecumbe when a sudden sensation of excitement rippled through him. "I knew that something psychic was about to happen, and I was concerned because driving down the highway at fifty-five miles an hour and having a vision is not a good idea."

He was only a few miles from his home and concentrated on his driving. As soon as he pulled into his carport, he turned off the engine and started to relax. His body went limp and he slumped in his seat. He turned his head slightly to the left and looked down onto the gray carport floor. "I felt like I was floating on a cloud and looking down into a gray abyss."

He kept his eyes open even though it seemed like he was dreaming. Suddenly, a vision appeared before him and he could see it crystal clear. It was like watching a television screen that was playing a movie. After a few moments, he realized that the television was part of the vision. He was watching an elderly man with gray, thinning hair and glasses, who seemed to be the host of a television show. He looked familiar, but Gernon didn't recognize him.

Suddenly, Gernon saw himself on the screen and realized that the man was introducing him. Maybe it was a fantasy, but it seemed that the man was giving him an opportunity to tell the world about the space-time warp he experienced on his flight in 1970. The vision lasted nearly five minutes and besides the interview he saw himself flying around what appeared to be the Florida Keys in an unfamiliar airplane. When the vision faded, he felt elated as if he'd just awakened from a special dream.

Almost three years later, in late 1994, Granite Film & Television Productions Company contacted Gernon. They told him that Arthur C. Clarke wanted him to appear on his television series, *Arthur C. Clarke's Mysterious Universe*. "That was when I realized that I'd already seen the show in my vision," Gernon recalled.

Clarke's film crew arrived from London several weeks later. They used Gernon's airplane, which he'd purchased the year before, to film the aerial shots for the documentary. The program appeared on the Discovery Channel and was called *Squaring the Bermuda Triangle*. "I can't recall all the details of the vision, but what I can remember was just like the television show."

How was it possible for Gernon to see something that wouldn't take place for several years? John Gribbin, author of *Timewarps*, sees a relationship between precognition and science's understanding of time and space. He notes that time doesn't move forward at a steady pace, but can be distorted or warped. "The evidence that some form of ill-understood mental process is able to short-circuit the normal 'causal' flow of time, and that this process works most effectively in providing some of us with 'precognitive' dreams, is now compelling." He says that these precognitive glimpses may represent mysterious resonances between individual minds, separated in time, but still able to exchange detailed information about specific events.

In the early 1990s, Gernon had another startling vision, but knows that he won't have the satisfaction of seeing it come true. That's because the event takes place in a museum years after he has died. It came to him in a lucid dream, one that feels particularly realistic and in which it seems that the dreamer is awake and dreaming at the same time. In this case, he glimpsed a future audience viewing a holographic depiction of his flight through the mother storm, into the electronic fog, and experiencing the space/time warp.

"The holograph was incredibly detailed, much more advanced than current technology offers." Gernon thinks the event was taking place sometime after the middle of the twenty-first century when the fog and its mysterious attributes has become an accepted reality and holographic images appear lifelike.

But precognition, as you'll see, isn't the only psychic talent that was developed by someone who survived an encounter with electronic fog.

Mind Over Windmills

One day in the fall of 2000, Bruce Gernon noticed an article in the *Palm Beach Post* about a writer who had coauthored a novel with actor Billy Dee Williams. When he saw that Rob MacGregor, like himself, lived in the village of Wellington, Florida, he felt an urge to contact him. At the same time, he figured that the writer wouldn't be interested in his story. Nevertheless he contacted him.

When they met, Gernon talked at length about his Bermuda Triangle experience. MacGregor was open-minded on the subject, but hesitant to do anything with the story because of other commitments. They kept in touch, though, and noted a number of odd coincidences that suggested they were destined to work together. Not only did they live just a couple of miles apart, but years ago MacGregor had interviewed Charles Berlitz, author of two best-selling books on the Bermuda Triangle, for a magazine article and Berlitz had given him a signed copy of *The Bermuda Triangle*.

Later, Gernon found out that MacGregor had also met the late pilot-author Martin Caidin, whose description of a flight through what sounded like electronic fog helped Gernon come to understand a key element of its nature, that the fog clings to objects. MacGregor told a peculiar story about Caidin that suggested that, like Gernon, Caidin had developed some unusual talents in the aftermath of his experience with the fog.

MacGregor and Caidin met, appropriately, at a bookstore. They were among several writers who participated in a group book signing event in support of a Gainesville, Florida, bookstore, which city officials were threatening to shut down for selling X-rated comic books.

During the event, Caidin was boisterous and opinionated. The bald-headed pilot in his early sixties with a big droopy mustache and large glasses dominated much of the conversation. Rather than a signing, at times it seemed that Caidin was holding court. Near the end of the event, he told the other writers about experiments he was conducting that involved psychokinetic energy. He invited, or rather challenged them, to come to his house to see for themselves. MacGregor and his wife, novelist T. J. MacGregor, were the only ones who took him up on the offer.

Even though Caidin had seemed somewhat boorish at the signing, he and his wife Dee Dee were gracious hosts. Caidin talked about his experiences as a pilot and emphasized the many strange incidents that had occurred to him. Although MacGregor can't recall all the details of their conversation, he thinks Caidin mentioned his flight through seemingly endless fog when none of the instruments worked.

But the main event of the evening was the experiment. Caidin was convinced that he possessed psychokinetic power, the ability to mentally move objects. In order to create an environment for his experiment, he had turned a large walk-in closet into a laboratory with a picture window. Viewing the lab through the window, MacGregor saw a table on which rested at least two dozen lightweight aluminum windmills, each one from six-to-eight inches tall. Caidin explained that the room was airtight and that the air-conditioning vent was sealed closed so that no air currents circulated through the room.

Caidin approached the window and began concentrating. Within a few seconds, two or three of the windmills began to slowly revolve. Then others joined and they picked up speed. Surprisingly, some of the vanes rotated clockwise, while others moved counterclockwise. A few of the windmills didn't move at all.

Caidin explained how a physics professor from the University of Florida had witnessed the experiments and closely examined the room, checking for any drafts. The professor had been impressed, but stopped short of acknowledging Caidin's ability, because Caidin, rather than a scientist, had created the laboratory.

Caidin claimed there was nothing psychic or paranormal about his abilities. He didn't like those terms. "The fact is, some people, including myself, can focus their mental powers and move objects. Mind over matter."

Did Caidin's ability relate directly to his experience in electronic fog? Maybe. His experience puts a new light on the story of the young German girl named Mina, who supposedly can move small objects with her mind. According to the account (see chapter 6), she was born at sea in the Bermuda Triangle during a forty-five-minute period when everyone on board felt confused and disoriented. Considering that Gernon's story, published in the same tabloid, was accurate, the same could be the case for Mina. Since Gernon wasn't interviewed, it was probably lifted from another publication, and the same might be true for Mina's story.

Regardless, the long-term effects on survivors of the fog, like Gernon and Caidin, need more scrutiny. That will happen as others who have experienced the fog come forward with their stories and, possibly, with their unusual mental talents, and when scientists put curiosity ahead of the fear of ridicule.

Measuring the Fog

Reflecting back on his journey through a tunnel in a storm cloud, Bruce Gernon had no idea that his decision would set off events that would change the way he looked at the world. "The reason I flew through it was because I saw blue sky on the other side. But then everything turned gray as I exited the tunnel."

Before the flight was over, he'd experienced a sense of zero gravity for about ten seconds, an apparent massive bank of fog that didn't appear on radar, failure of all his electronic equipment, and a time distortion. It would take him thirty years before he would realize that there was no huge bank of fog spanning mile after mile, that the fog only surrounded his plane and was clinging to it.

Gernon is now convinced that a mysterious meteorological phenomenon—electronic fog—is responsible for some of the baffling incidents reported by pilots—including himself, Charles Lindbergh, and aeronautics author Martin Caidin—as well as pilots and sailors both inside and outside the Bermuda Triangle. To that end, he has devised a five-level scale to describe the various stages of electronic fog, which seemingly attaches itself to passing crafts. He has experienced two of the levels himself in his numerous Caribbean-South Florida flights.

The essence of Gernon's contention is that the relationship between flying or sailing crafts and electronic fog is somewhat similar to a magnet and a piece of iron. Essentially, when pilots or sailors encounter electronic fog, they believe they are flying or sailing through a vast area of haze when in reality the fog is localized. The fog, he realized, reacts to the aircraft just as lightning is drawn to the tallest object in its path. Electronic fog literally attaches to passing aircraft as if it were hitching a ride. So in spite of the illusion of flying mile after mile through a fog, the fog actually accompanies the pilot. In doing so, it sometimes caused electronic equipment to malfunction often sending pilots to their deaths. In some instances, it even hurtled the craft, pilot, and passengers forward or backward in time.

Here is a description of the scale, which is oriented toward aircrafts.

The Gernon Scale of Electronic Fog

1. Appears as a mist or haze with visibility of between two and three miles. Magnetic and electronic navigational equipment are not effected, but the fog clings to the plane.

2. Creates the illusion that it rises from the surface and spreads out for an unlimited distance below the craft. The sky is clear above the aircraft. A tunnel or shaft may appear directly below the aircraft revealing the earth. Vis-

ibility is near zero within the fog with the exception of the shaft. Magnetic and electronic navigational equipment is not affected.

3. Completely surrounds the aircraft with the exception of two shafts—one above and one below the plane. Visibility is near zero in the fog and unlimited in the shaft. Magnetic and navigational equipment *will* malfunction, including radios after a period of time.

4. Surrounds aircraft with visibility severely limited and obscured to shades of gray. Visibility appears to be from one to two miles. The sun or moon will not be visible but can be determined by the intensity of brightness. Landmarks may be identified but will appear hazy. Elec tronic and navigational equipment will malfunction, but radios will work, at least for the first few minutes. Space-time warps may take effect.

5. Appears to envelop the aircraft with visibility totally obscured. Magnetic and navigational equipment failure including radios. Space-time warps occur instantaneously upon entry and induce total disintegration of aircraft and its occupants.

Gernon believes that electronic fog is an outgrowth of a powerful electromagnetic storm, one that materializes suddenly, then disappears. Pilots might enter a Category 1 electronic fog and experience only a haze or mist, nothing that seems out of the ordinary. When pilots enter a Category 2 or 3 electronic fog, they probably won't see the mother storm, either. That was the case with Gernon in his second encounter with electronic fog in 1996, a flight from the Florida Keys described in chapter 6.

While pilots caught in a Category 2 or 3 fog see only the haze, the mother storm itself is enormous and short-lived. The storm, Gernon attests from his own experience in 1970, materializes at an incredibly rapid rate of 300 miles per hour, expanding out to a diameter of thirty miles and up from the ocean surface to an altitude of 40,000 feet within twenty minutes. Amazingly, it dissipates within half an hour of its birth. Noting its short life, Gernon says he knows of no other pilot who has seen this storm from its birth, fly directly through the heart of it, and exit through what he calls a time tunnel vortex.

At that point, he was enveloped by electronic fog of a Category 4 level on his scale. If others have duplicated Gernon's feat, they might not have survived to tell about it.

Shortly after the dramatic incident, Gernon talked to a meteorologist at Miami Flight Service and told him about the unusual fog that was undetected by radar. He asked for an explanation, but none was forthcoming. "He found the story fascinating, but he couldn't explain it," Gernon recalled. Or could anyone else.

———————

Meteorologists recognize the existence of magnetic anomalies in the Caribbean and elsewhere on the planet. They also acknowledge that static electricity from electromagnetic storms can knock out electronic instruments in airplanes. However, at present, they don't recognize the existence of electronic fog, much less Gernon's scale.

Gernon, however, points out that science couldn't explain the phenomena of electricity until the late eighteenth century even though various manifestations of the electricity had been known since antiquity. Likewise, until 1802, scientists adamantly refused to accept the existence of meteors, because it conflicted with the scientific paradigm of the time. Rocks did not fall from the sky. That was simply superstition. Yet, there had been abundant evidence going back centuries that rocks *did* indeed fall from the sky. Eventually, scientific proof was obtained and the existence of meteors was accepted.

Today, scientists say that fog doesn't "stick" to airplanes and there are no time tunnels that airplanes can fly through. Gernon, though, is convinced that eventually electronic fog will shift from anomalous experience into scientific fact in the same way that we now recognize electricity and meteors. He also thinks that time distortions related to electronic fog and electromagnetic energy fields may become a fact in the same sense that we have harnessed electricity.

But what about Category 5 of the scale? Does it really exist? Could a pilot and his airplane literally vanish into another time? Is that what happened to Flight 19?

Gernon is cautious and thoughtful when he answers that question. He's convinced that Flight 19 did enter electronic fog before disappearing. Electronic equipment malfunctioned. The pilots became disoriented and lost.

The situation reminds him of his own flight in the same area of the Caribbean. When the radar controller told him to identify himself with his transponder, the controller was unable to locate him. Instead of having only a single electric homing device, like Flight 19, Gernon had three on board and all three malfunctioned.

"During the time that I was in the electronic fog, I wasn't on radar and it was impossible to obtain a heading toward Miami or Fort Lauderdale. This seems to me to be the same situation that Flight 19 was experiencing at the same time as me, and almost in the same location, only twenty-five years earlier."

So where did Flight 19 end up?

Category 5 electronic fog experience is not only hypothetical, but virtually impossible to prove. There are no survivors, no documentation. So as a plane enters Category 5 electronic fog, the pilot literally flies into the mythical Bermuda Triangle, a place that may exist more in the mind than in physical reality.

Gernon speculates that if he had flown in the opposite direction through the tunnel in his 1970 flight, either his plane would've disintegrated or he would have entered a time warp to the past, rather than the future, and probably wouldn't have survived. The same could be suggested about the fate of Flight 19.

Yet, Gernon isn't so sure about that. He concedes that Flight 19 might simply have crashed far out in the Atlantic after the planes ran out of gas. Rather than lost in the past, Flight 19 is probably resting in the depths a couple miles below the ocean surface. In fact, he predicts that, like the Titanic, the five Avengers eventually will be found with the help of technological advances in deep-water scanning devices that are now available.

––––––––––

If electronic fog became a scientific reality, would it be possible to "capture" or create such energy the way that we have harnessed electricity? Is the government already quietly working on such projects in secretive bases, perhaps at AUTEC? Gernon recognizes that the subject is controversial, that time travel windows currently exist only in the realm of science fiction, but he's convinced that situation will change.

If he is right, our worldview, of course, would be greatly altered. Harnessing time travel to the future would change our approach to decision-making. It would transform the world just as electricity now illuminates the night and powers virtually everything.

Let's take a brief journey into that world. Imagine this scenario: The U.S. government is contemplating attacking a dangerous foreign nation with a crazed leader who is threatening to set off a nuclear weapon. The U.S. Congress now has access to possible future events. They program a decision to attack and study the most likely results of such an action. They could go ahead one year, five years, or ten years. If the futility of the war was documented, it could be averted. However, if it appeared that a lack of action would result in the destruction of the Western world, Congress could authorize an attack.

Like atomic energy, the power to enter the future could be used for good or evil purposes, depending on who was making the decisions. Maybe the reason that scientists haven't recognized electronic fog and its link to time travel is because we're not yet ready for it. Maybe it will remain the realm of science fiction until the human race evolves far enough along its path to deal with the awesome powers that would result from the ability to open the door to the future at will.

That doorway might lead to something altogether unexpected. If we could move at will to the future or past, in the same way that we might send a crew on the space shuttle or even on a supersonic jet, humanity, at that point, might be on the verge of freeing itself from the restrictions of time and space. In that world, we would recognize that the past, present, and future unravels simultaneously.

We could become like the gods of the past. In fact, it might turn out that we were—or rather will be—the gods who resided on Mount Olympus and elsewhere in our mythological past.

Vanishing Ships

Some of the disappearances of sailing vessels date back to the seventeenth century. Two of the lost ships were more than five-hundred feet long. Some of these vessels may have vanished in inclement weather, but many disappeared on calm days. Most never had time to send out a mayday. No war-related disappearances are included.

1609: The *Sea Venture* and its rescue boat were lost off the coast of Bermuda.

1750: *Nuestra Senora de Guadalupe*'s three accompanying galleons vanished off the North Carolina coast.

1780: *Saratoga*, a military vessel, mysteriously vanished; no British warships claimed sinking her. That same year the *General Gates* was lost and again no British warship took credit for sinking her.

1799: U.S.S. *Insurgent*, a thirty-six-gun French-built warship, disappeared with a crew of 340.

1800: U.S.S. *Pickering* disappeared on a voyage to the West Indies.

1812: *Patriot,* a packet ship carrying Aaron Burr's daughter disappeared in the Gulf Stream.

1814: *Wasp,* a U.S. warship, disappeared off the coast of South Carolina.

1815: The *Epervier* carried the peace proposals for the War of 1812 on a voyage from Algiers to Norfolk. The ship never arrived, hence delaying the end of the war.

1824: The *Wildcat* with a crew of thirty-one, the schooner *Lynx* carrying forty sailors, and the schooner *Hornet* all vanished in or near the area designated as the Bermuda Triangle.

1840: The merchant ship, *Rosalie,* vanished in the Sargasso Sea. There were reports that the ship was derelict.

1843: The warship *Grampas* sailed south of the Carolinas and was never seen again.

1854: The passenger vessel *City of Glasgow* went missing with its four hundred passengers as it took a southern route out of New York to Liverpool.

1872: *Mary Celeste* was found adrift without its crew.

1880: The British training brig HMS *Atalanta* departed from Bermuda with 290 young cadets and was never seen again.

1909: Joshua Slocum sailed *The Spray,* a sloop, out of Miami and vanished. Slocum, a world circumnavigator, was considered among the best sailors of his day.

1917: The freighter *Timandra,* bound for Buenos Aires from Norfolk, disappeared between March 6 and March 27 with a crew of twenty-one and a cargo of coal.

1918: The 542-foot-long USS *Cyclops*, the largest ship in the navy, vanished after March 6 with a crew of 306 after leaving Barbados en route to Virginia.

1921: *Carroll Deering*, a five-masted schooner, left Barbados en route to Virginia and was found afloat without its crew.

1925: The tramp steamer *Cotopaxi* vanished December 1 with a crew of thirty-two en route to Havana from Charleston, South Carolina.

1926: *Porta Noca*, a passenger ship, departed from Cuba and was never seen again.

The freighter *Suduffco* sailed from New York to Los Angeles in March with four thousand tons of cargo and a crew of twenty-nine, but never reached Panama.

1931: *Stavenger*, a freighter, lost with crew of forty-three.

1932: Two-masted sailing vessel *John and Mary*, vanished.

1938: The freighter *Anglo-Australian* disappeared with a crew of thirty-nine; she was last reported off the Azores.

1940: The schooner *Gloria Colite* was discovered February 4 without a crew; the craft was still seaworthy.

1946: The schooner *City Belle* was found derelict December 5 in the Bahamas; its ten passengers and crew missing.

1948: The *Evelyn K.* was found deserted March 6 in the Florida Keys; three people missing.

1950: the 185-foot coaster *Sandra*, with a cargo of DDT, vanished April 5 en route to Venezuela from Savannah, Georgia.

1955: Yacht *Connemara IV* was discovered September 26 intact with no crew 150 miles southeast of Bermuda.

The yacht *Home Sweet Home* vanished January 13 en route from Bermuda to St. Thomas.

1956: The schooner *Bounty* disappeared in July between Bimini and Miami.

1958: The yacht *Renovoc,* with a crew of four, vanished January 1 after leaving Key West.

1960: The yacht *Ethel C.* went missing April 16, off Virginia.

1961: The yacht *Callista III* disappeared April 5 en route to the Bahamas.

1962: The schooner *Evangeline* vanished.

The *Windfall,* a 56-foot schooner on its way to the Bahamas, went missing in November with a crew of five.

1963: The *Marine Sulphur Queen,* a 504-foot American freighter, was lost February 4 in the Florida Straits with a crew of thirty-nine.

A fishing vessel *Sno Boy* disappeared July 2 between Kingston and Northeast Cay.

1964: The thirty-six-foot ketch *Dancing Feathers* vanished en route to the Bahamas.

1965: The fifty-eight-foot *Enchantress* was last heard from January 13, approximately 150 miles southeast of Charleston, South Carolina.

A houseboat, *El Gato*, vanished October 28 near Great Inagua, Bahamas.

1967: *Speed Artist* disappeared December 10, with a crew of five, near the Windward Islands.

A cabin cruiser, *Witchcraft*, disappeared December 22 off Miami.

1968: The *Scorpion*, a nuclear-powered submarine, was lost.

1969: The yacht *Vagabond* was found derelict July 12 at the edge of the Sargasso Sea.

The cabin cruiser *Southern Cross* was found November 2 deserted off Cape May.

1971: The 339-foot cargo vessel *El Caribe*, was lost October 10, in the Caribbean.

1973: The 541-foot German freighter *Anita*, was lost March 21 in heavy seas with crew of thirty-two.

The eighty-eight-foot yacht *Defiance* was found derelict March 23, near Cap du Mole, St. Nicholas, Haiti.

1974: A fifty-four-foot luxury yacht *Saba Bank* disappeared in March, while cruising the Bahamas.

A yacht, *Dutch Treat*, disappeared July 24 en route from Miami to Cat Cay, Bahamas.

1975: A seventy-three-foot shrimper, *Dawn*, vanished April 22 near Smith Shoals, Key West.

A yacht, *Meridian*, bound to Bermuda from Norfolk, vanished June 24.

An ocean-going tug, *Boundless*, disappeared December 2 in the Bahamas.

1976: A motorized sailing vessel, *High Flight*, disappeared in April between Bimini and Miami.

The 590-foot ore carrier *Sylvia L. Ossa*, was lost in October about 140 miles west of Bermuda with a crew of thirty-seven.

A forty-foot sloop with seventeen people aboard vanished December 16 between St. Kitts and Dominica.

1977: The schooner *L'Avenir* disappeared November 20 en route to Bermuda from Maryland.

1979: A sixty-six-foot tug, *King Cobra*, vanished January 2 near Cape Henlopen, Delaware.

1980: The *Sea Quest* sent out a mysterious call January 12, saying its navigational equipment wasn't working. After that call, nothing was heard or seen of the vessel with eleven people aboard.

A forty-three-foot luxury yacht, *Polymer III*, was lost in April while cruising the Bahamas.

A thirty-eight-foot sailboat, *Kalia III*, was found derelict July 26 in the Exumas, Bahamas.

The 520-foot *S.S. Poet* went missing October 26 after departing from Cape Henlopen en route to Port Said, Egypt.

1982: American yacht *Penetration* found July 26 deserted north of Sargasso Sea.

A British yacht was found deserted in the Atlantic.

The forty-four-foot *Sea Lure* disappeared February 26 from a group of fishing vessels while headed toward Dry Tortugas.

1983: The thirty-two-foot sport fishing boat *Real Fine*, disappeared November 5 and 6 en route from Freeport, the Bahamas, to Fort Lauderdale.

1984: A seventeen-foot motor boat with four people aboard disappeared November 22 near Looe Key Reef in the Florida Keys.

1985: A twenty-five-foot pleasure boat, with two aboard, disappeared February 22 en route from Freeport to West Palm Beach.

Six persons disappeared May 3 in an outboard off Surf City, North Carolina.

1992: A fishing vessel, *Mae Doris*, vanished October 27 with crew of four, south of Cape May.

1995: The *Jamanic K*, a motorboat, went missing March 20 en route from Cape Haitien to Miami.

A sailboat, *Fou de Bassan III* was found derelict December 19.

1996: A sixty-five-foot yacht, *Intrepid*, disappeared October 14 about thirty miles off Fort Pierce, Florida, with sixteen people aboard. A brief mayday call was picked up.

1997: The twenty-three-foot *Robalo*, disappeared in December off Virginia Beach, Virginia.

1998: A commercial fishing vessel, *Grumpy*, was found derelict January 2.

A thirty-five-foot converted sport fishing vessel, *Miss Charlotte*, was hit by a strong force on May 1, possibly a waterspout, which cleared the deck. The vessel sunk, but the crew survived.

The *Carolina* disappeared in November off Cape May.

The seventy-four-foot *Interlude* vanished in November during cruise to the Cayman Islands.

1999: *Miss Fernandina*, an eighty-five-foot shrimp trawler, disappeared April 15 off Flagler Beach, Florida. The captain radioed for help, saying that a net was caught in the propeller.

An eighteen-foot day cruiser was found derelict August 5, except for its dog. The skipper was on a two-hour cruise off the North Carolina coast.

A twenty-two-foot day cruiser vanished November 15 in the Bahamas.

2000: A freighter, en route to Haiti, vanished, but the cargo floated ashore to Florida.

Vanishing Airplanes

More airplanes vanished in the Caribbean in the 1970s, when the Bermuda Triangle was gaining its notoriety, than in any other decade before or since. The first five airplanes to disappear in the Caribbean, lost during the same flight, set off the Bermuda Triangle mystery. The *Star Tiger* and *Star Aerial* were sister crafts and vanished in the Bermuda Triangle within a year of each other. A DC3 owned by Argosy Airlines vanished in 1978, and it was an article in *Argosy* magazine where the name Bermuda Triangle first appeared.

1945: Five U.S. Navy *Avenger* bombers, Flight 19, disappeared December 5 with a crew of fourteen followed by the loss of a rescue plane, a Martin Mariner with a crew of thirteen.

1947: An army C-54 Douglas Superfort vanished July 3 about a hundred miles off Bermuda with a crew of seven.

1948: A Douglas DC-3 airliner, carrying thirty-one passengers and crew members, disappeared December 28 at sea on its approach to Miami.

Star Tiger, a British commercial airliner, a four-engined Tudor IV, disappeared January 30 with a crew of thirty-one on a flight to Bermuda from the Azores.

1949: *Star Ariel*, another Tudor IV and the sister ship of the *Star Tiger*, vanished January 17 en route to Kingston with nineteen aboard.

1952: A British York transport plane, lost with a crew of thirty-three.

1954: U.S. Navy Lockheed Super Constellation vanished October 30 with forty-two aboard.

1956: U.S. Navy seaplane *Martin Marlin PSM*, an amphibious patrol plane, disappeared November 9 with a crew of ten about 350 miles north of Bermuda.

1961: An eight-engine SAC B-52, *Pogo 22*, vanished October 15 north of Bermuda while returning from routine maneuvers.

1962: A private plane disappeared off Nassau.

U.S. Air Force KB-50 aerial tanker plane lost January 8 with a crew of eight en route from North Carolia to the Azores.

U.S. Air Force Tender vanished en route to Azores.

A C-133 Cargomaster with a crew of ten disappeared May 27 en route from Dover, England to the Azores.

1963: Two U.S. Air Force giant Stratotankers disintegrated August 28 on a simple exercise as they flew to Miami from Bermuda with a ten-person crew.

Another C-133 Cargomaster vanished September 22 en route to the Azores from Dover.

1964: A Piper Apache was lost February 8 with four aboard, between Grand Bahama Island and West Palm Beach, Florida.

A Cessna 140 with two persons aboard disappeared December 5 off New Smyrna Beach, Florida.

1965: A C-119 Flying Boxcar disappeared June 5 with crew of ten, en route from Miami to Grand Turks.

A Beechcraft C18s with three persons aboard vanished September 15 near St. Thomas.

Cessna 182 disappeared with two aboard on October 31, somewhere between Marathon Key and Key West, Florida.

An Ercoupe F01 was lost with two persons aboard, between Fort Lauderdale and West End, Grand Bahama on December 6.

A Piper Cherokee, flying from South Caicos for San Juan, disappeared December 29 with three persons aboard.

1966: A converted cargo B-25 vanished April 5 en route from Fort Lauderdale to Aruba.

1967: A military YC-122, converted to cargo plane, disappeared between Fort Lauderdale and Bimini on January 11.

A Beechcraft Bonanza was lost near Key Largo on January 14, with four aboard.

A Piper Cherokee en route to St. Thomas from San Juan disappeared January 17.

A Cherokee near Mayaguez, Puerto Rico, vanished on July 2 with four aboard.

A Piper Cherokee disappeared between Miami and Bimini on August 6, with three aboard.

A Cherokee traveling from Great Inagua and San Juan vanished on October 3.

A Cessna 182 vanished on November 8 en route to Nassau from Great Exuma with four aboard.

A Cherokee disappeared near Cat Island, Bahamas with four aboard on November 22.

1968: A Cessna 172 with two aboard disappeared near Grand Turk on May 29.

A Cessna 180 flying to West Palm Beach from Grand Bahama disappeared July 8 with two aboard.

1969: A Piper Comanche flying from Pompano Beach to North Carolina disappeared with two aboard over the Caribbean January 5.

A Beechcraft 95-C55, en route Miami from Georgia, disappeared February 15.

A Douglas DC-4 cargo plane vanished after leaving the Azores on March 8, with a crew of three.

A Beechcraft disappeared between Jamaica and Nassau March 22 with two aboard.

A Cessna 172 went missing between Grand Turk and Caicos Island on June 6 with two aboard.

A B-95 Beechcraft Executive disappeared on June 29 while flying from Great Inagua for San Juan.

A Piper PA-22 en route from West Palm Beach to Albion, New Jersey, vanished August 3, with two persons aboard.

On October 11, a Pilattus-Brittan-Norman Islander with two aboard was lost on a flight from Great Inagua for Puerto Rico.

1970: A Piper Comanche with two aboard vanished between Nassau and Opa Locka, Florida, on January 17.

A Cessna 310G with six aboard was lost on July 3 between Caracus, Venezuela, and San Juan.

On November 23, a Piper Comanche disappeared between West Palm Beach and Kingston, Jamaica, with three persons aboard.

1971: A pilot and his Cessna 177B vanished on March 20 en route to Andros Island from Miami.

A Horizon Hunter Club's rental plane disappeared March 20 near Barbados with four aboard.

On September 10, a Phantom II F-4E jet, with two pilots, vanished during routine maneuvers eighty-two miles south of Miami.

A pilot and his Cessna 150J disappeared after leaving Pompano Beach, destination unknown.

1972: A Super Constellation with a crew of four were lost October 10 between Miami and Santo Domingo.

1973: A pilot and a Cessna 172 disappeared March 28 after leaving West Palm Beach.

A Navion A16 was lost May 25 between Freeport and West Palm Beach, with two aboard.

A Beechcraft Bonanza vanished between Fort Lauderdale and Marsh Harbour, Bahamas, on August 10 with four persons aboard.

After departing from Viaquez, Puerto Rico, a Cessna 150 vanished with three aboard.

A Lake Amphibian was lost December 20 between Nassau and Bimini with three persons aboard.

1974: A pilot and his Cessna 414 vanished February 10 after leaving Treasure Cay, Bahamas.

On February 10, a Pilattus-Brittan-Norman Islander with two aboard disappeared on the approach St. Thomas.

A Piper PA-32 vanished between West Palm Beach and Walker Cay, Bahamas, on July 13.

A Beech K35 Bonanza was lost after departing from Pompano Beach en route to Philadelphia on August 11 with two aboard.

1975: A pilot and his Piper PA-30 en route to Freeport, Grand Bahamas, from Greensboro, North Carolina, disappeared February 25.

A pilot flew his Cessna "Skymaster" out of Fort Lauderdale on May 2 and was lost at sea.

A pilot and his Cessna 172 disappeared, July 28 in the vicinity of Fort Lauderdale.

A pilot and his Cessna 172 were lost between St. Croix and St. Kitts on December 9.

1976: A Beech D50 with two aboard vanished en route to the Dominican Republic from Pahokee, Florida, on June 4.

A Beech E-50, flying from Opa Locka, Florida, to Grand Turk Island, disappeared on October 24.

A Piper PA-23, flying from Anguilla to Beef Island, vanished December 28 with six aboard.

1978: On February 22, a KA-6 Navy attack bomber with two aboard vanished from radar a hundred miles off Norfolk en route to the U.S.S. *John F. Kennedy*.

An Aero Commander 680 flying from Imokalee, Florida, to Freeport to Freeport, Grand Bahama, disappeared March 25 with two aboard.

A pilot flying a Ted Smith 601 from Pompano Beach to Panama City, Florida, disappeared on April 27.

A pilot and his Cessna 172 was lost on April 30 after departing from Dillon, South Carolina.

A Piper PA-28, flying from Fort Pierce to Nassau, on May 19 disappeared with four aboard.

A Beech 65, flying from Port-au-Prince to the Bahamas, vanished on May 26 with two aboard.

A Piper PA-31, en route from Santa Marta, Colombia, to Port-au-Prince, vanished on July 18 with two aboard.

A Douglas DC-3, flying from Fort Lauderdale to Havana, disappeared on September 21 with four aboard.

A Douglas DC-3, Argosy Airlines Flight 902, disappeared off Miami.

A pilot and his Piper PA-31, flying from St. Croix to St. Thomas, vanished on the approach to the island on November 3.

A Piper PA-23, flying from De Funiak Springs to Gainsville, Florida, disappeared on November 20 with four aboard.

Eastern Caribbean Airlines Flight 912 vanished on approach to airport on St. Thomas. No wreckage was found.

1979: A Cessna 150 was lost near St. Thomas; no debris found.

A Beech A23A, flying from Opa Locka, Florida to St. Thomas, disappeared January 11, with two aboard.

A pilot and his Beech E18S, en route from Fort Lauderdale to Cat Island, Bahamas, was lost on April 2.

A Piper PA-28R, with four aboard, vanished April 24 en route to Nassau from Fort Lauderdale.

Cessna 150J, traveling from St. Croix to St. Thomas, disappeared June 30 with two aboard.

A Cessna 182 disappeared September 9 on a flight from New Orleans to Pensacola, with three persons aboard.

A pilot and his Aero Commander 500 vanished while flying from Andros Island to West Palm Beach on October 4.

A pilot and his Piper PA-23 were lost October 27 on a flight from Montego Bay, Jamaica, to Nassau.

A pilot and his Beech D50 vanished on November 19 en route to Key West from Delray Beach, Florida.

A Piper PA-23 disappeared on a flight from Aguadilla, Puerto Rico, to South Caicos Island on December 21 with four persons aboard.

1980: A pilot took off in a Beech 58 from St. Thomas on February 11 and vanished. The aircraft was reported as stolen.

A Lear jet disappeared with two aboard May 19 after taking off from West Palm Beach en route to New Orleans.

A Erco 415 with two persons aboard vanished June 28 on a flight from Santo Domingo, Dominican Republic, to San Juan, Puerto Rico. The pilot reported seeing a UFO before disappearing.

1981: A Beech C35 flying from Bimini to Nassau disappeared on January 6. with four aboard.

1982: A Piper PA-28R-201T en route from Nashville to Venice, Florida. Vanished July 5 with four aboard.

A Beech H35 en route to Fort Pierce, Florida, from Marsh Harbour disappeared September 28 with two aboard.

A Piper PA-31, with eight aboard, vanished October 20 en route to St. Thomas from Anguilla with eight persons aboard.

A Beech 65-B80, flying from Fort Lauderdale to Eleuthera Island, Bahamas, disappeared November 5 with three persons aboard.

1983: A Cessna T-210-J en route from Andros Island to Fort Pierce, Florida, disappeared October 4 with three aboard.

On November 20, a pilot and his Cessna 340A disappeared near Orangeville, Florida.

1984: A Piper, with four persons aboard, vanished on March 12 between Key West and Clearwater.

A Cessna 402B disappeared on March 31 between Fort Lauderdale and Bimini with six aboard.

A pilot and his Aeronca 7AC was lost on December 23 between Cross City, Florida, and Alabama.

1985: A Cessna 337, with four aboard, disappeared in the Atlantic northeast of Jacksonville on January 14.

A pilot and his Cessna 210K, en route from Miami to Port-au-Prince, vanished on May 8.

A Piper disappeared July 12 on a flight from Nassau to Opa-Locka, Florida, with four aboard.

On August 3, a pilot and his Cessna 172 disappeared near Fort Myers, Florida.

On September 8, a Piper vanished northeast of Key West on a flight from Fort Lauderdale, with two aboard.

A pilot and his Piper disappeared on October 31 between Sarasota, Florida, and Columbus, Georgia.

1986: A Piper en route from Miami to West End or Freeport, Grand Bahamas, vanished on March 26 with six aboard.

A Twin Otter charter disappeared on August 3 near St. Vincent with thirteen people aboard.

1987: A pilot and his Cessna 402C vanished between Palm Beach and Marsh Harbour, Great Abaco, on May 27.

A Cessna 401, en route from Freeport to Crooked Island, disappeared on June 3 with four aboard.

A pilot and his Cessna 152 vanished December 2 on a flight from La Romana, Puerto Rico, to nearby San Juan.

1988: A Beechcraft disappeared on February 7, somewhere over the Caribbean, with four persons aboard.

1989: After departing from Jacksonville on February 6, a pilot and his Piper disappeared.

1990: A Cessna 152, with two aboard, vanished January 24 on an instructional flight near West Palm Beach.

A pilot and his Piper disappeared June 5, on a flight from St. Maarten to St. Croix.

A Piper vanished on August 10 between Sebastian, Florida, and Freeport with four aboard. A body of one of the occupants was later discovered off the coast of Virginia.

Cherokee 150 disappeared on approach to St. Croix; no trace of plane or passengers found.

1991: A pilot and his Piper Comanche vanished April 24 off the Florida coast.

A pilot of a Piper indicated that his directional gyro wasn't working. The plane with two aboard fell off radar near Long Boat Key.

A Grumman Cougar jet with two aboard disappeared from radar over the Gulf of Mexico October 31 as it climbed to 25,300 feet.

1993: A pilot and his Cessna 152 disappeared September 30 off the coast of Miami.

1994: A Piper PA-32 with two aboard vanished August 28 on a flight from Treasure Cay, Bahamas, to Fort Pierce with two aboard.

A Piper PA-23, with five aboard, vanished September 19 over the Caribbean, after departing from the Canefield airport in the Dominican Republic.

A pilot and his Piper PA-28 vanished on Christmas Day flight originating in Boca Raton, Florida.

1996: A chartered Aero Commander was lost over the Caribbean on May 2 with three aboard.

1998: A Piper PA-28, with four aboard, disappeared August 19.

1999: On May 12, a pilot and his Aero Commander 500B nose-dived into sea, in clear skies, near Nassau, after radioing tower for landing instructions.

2000: A Cessna 172 crashed into sea when the pilot couldn't find well-lit airport.

2001: A pilot and his Piper Archer crashed off Florida Keys after encountering localized fog that a coast guard aircraft could not see.

2002: Piper Lance II disappeared on July 20 off Grand Bahama with six aboard.

A pilot flying a Piper PA-36-300 was lost September 6 on a flight from Fort Lauderdale to St. Croix.

Where Was Atlantis?

Here are some of the geographic regions where Atlantis has been located through the ages:

370 B.C.: Plato, philosopher, Greek scholar—Beyond the pillars of Hercules (Gibraltar, west of the Mediterranean)

1500: Francesco Lopez de Gomara, Spanish scholar—The American continent

1570s: John Dee, astrologer, mathematician, and scientist—North America

1670s: Athanasius Kircher, Austrian Jesuit priest—Mid-Atlantic

1794: Paul Felix Cabrera, Guatemalan doctor—Haiti

1882: Ignatius Donnelly, U.S. Congressman—Mid-Atlantic

1909: K. T. Frost, Belfast scholar—Crete

1922: Adolf Schulten, German scientist—Tartessos, Spain

1920s: Lewis Spence, Scottish mythologist—Bahamas, as last landmass of Atlantis

1933: Edgar Cayce, American psychic—Bimini and the Bahamas as "Poseidia," a fragment of Atlantis that stretched across to the African coast

1969: A. G. Galanopoulos and E. Bacon, Aegean historians—Crete

1991: Emilio Spedicato, Professor at Bergamo University—Haiti

1995: Rose and Rand Flem-Ath, Canadian writers—Antarctica

1997: Viatcheslav Koudriavtsev, Russian scientist—Off west coast of Britain

2000: Andrew Collins, British historical writer—Cuba

2001: Jacques Collina-Girard, French geologist and prehistorian—In the Atlantic, west of Gibraltar.

Here are the most popular locations for Atlantis today, and the reasoning:

1. Antarctica—the icy continent was once above sea level
2. Mid-Atlantic—Lots of room
3. Bahamas—Edgar Cayce's prediction
4. Crete—archaeological and geologic evidence
5. Cuba—recent discoveries
6. Nowhere—Atlantis was a story

Bibliography

Barbour, Julian. *The End of Time: The Next Revolution in Physics*, New York: Oxford University Press, 2000.

Berlitz, Charles. *The Bermuda Triangle: An Incredible Saga of Unexplained Disappearances*, New York: Doubleday, 1974.

———. *Without a Trace*, New York: Doubleday, 1977.

Budden, Albert. *Electric UFOs: Fireballs, Electromagnetics, and Abnormal States*, London: Blandford, 1998.

Ebon, Martin. *The Riddle of the Bermuda Triangle*, New York: Signet, 1975.

Caidin, Martin. *Ghosts of the Air: True Stories of Aerial Hauntings*, New York: Bantam, 1991.

Corliss, William R. *Remarkable Luminous Phenomena in Nature: A Catalog of Geophysical Anomalies*, Glen Arm, MD: Sourcebook Project, 2001.

———. *Lightning, Auroras, Nocturnal Lights, and Related Luminous Phenomena*, Glen Arm, MD: Sourcebook Project, 1982.

Jeffrey, Adi-Ken Thomas. *The Bermuda Triangle*, New York: Warner Books, 1971.

Kusche, Larry. *The Bermuda Triangle Mystery–Solved*, Great Britain: New English Library, 1975.

———. *The Disappearance of Flight 19*, New York: Harper & Row, 1980.

Lindbergh, Charles. *Autobiography of Values*, New York: Harcourt, Brace, Jovanovich, 1977.

Quasar, Gian J. *Into the Bermuda Triangle: Pursuing the Truth Behind the World's Greatest Mystery*, Camden, ME: McGraw Hill, 2004.

Randles, Jenny. *Time Storms: Amazing Evidence for Time Warps, Space Rifts, and Time Travel*, New York: Berkley Books, 2002.

Smith, Warren, *Triangle of the Lost*, New York, Zebra, 1975.

Smoot, George and Keay Davidson. *Wrinkles in Time*, New York: Avon Books, 1993.

Spaeth, Frank. *Mysteries of the Deep: Amazing Phenomena in Our World's Waterways*, St. Paul, MN: Llewellyn Publications, 1998.

Tesla, Nikola and David H. Childress. *The Fantastic Inventions of Nikola Tesla*, Kempton, IL: Adventures Unlimited Press, 1993.

Index

Atlantis
Insights from a Lost Civilization

SHIRLEY ANDREWS

The legend of lost Atlantis turns to fact as Shirley Andrews uniquely correlates a wealth of information from more than 100 classical and Atlantean scholars, scientists, and psychics to describe the country and its inhabitants.

Review the scientific and geological evidence for an Atlantic continent, which refutes the popular notion that Atlantis was located in the Mediterranean. Follow the history of Atlantis from its beginnings to its destruction, and see a portrait of Atlantean society: its religion, architecture, art, medicine, and lifestyle. Learn what happened to the survivors of Atlantis, where they migrated, and how the survivors and their descendants made their mark on cultures the world over.

1-56718-023-X
272 pp., 6 x 9, illus. $12.95

Spanish edition:
Atlántida
0-7387-0563-2 $14.95

To order, call 1-877-NEW-WRLD
Prices subject to change without notice

Lemuria and Atlantis
Studying the Past to Survive the Future

<small>SHIRLEY ANDREWS</small>

Once again, Shirley Andrews (author of the popular *Atlantis: Insights from a Lost Civilization*) combines her own research with the data of scholars, scientists, and respected psychics to offer a compelling look into the little-known details about the lost continent of Lemuria and its relationship to Atlantis.

What was life like on this beautiful Pacific land before nature destroyed it in 10,000 B.C.? What relevance do these lost civilizations have for today's world? Andrews uncovers evidence of Atlanteans and Lemurians in the Americas, advanced technologies, vibrational healing methods, extraterrestrial intervention, human-animal hybrids, and other civilizations of prehistory.

0-7387-0397-4
288 pp., 6 x 9, maps $12.95

Spanish edition:
Lemuria y Atlántida
0-7387-0656-6 $14.95

To order, call 1-877-NEW-WRLD
<small>Prices subject to change without notice</small>

Strange But True

From the Files of FATE Magazine

CORRINE KENNER & CRAIG MILLER

Have you had a mystical experience? You're not alone. For almost fifty years, FATE readers have been reporting their encounters with the strange and unknown. In this collection, you'll meet loved ones who return from beyond the grave, mysterious voices warning of danger, guardian angels, and miraculous healings by benevolent forces. Every report is a firsthand account, complete with full details and vivid descriptions.

1-56718-298-4
256 pp., 5³⁄₁₆ x 8 $9.95

UFO Mysteries

A Reporter Seeks the Truth

CURT SUTHERLY

Take a weird journey into the unexplained with fifteen gripping stories gathered from the author's own journalistic investigations. From alien encounters to eyewitness disappearances to the Mars probe failure, these are puzzles without real solutions.

Curt Sutherly points out significant parallels among sightings in different parts of the United States, which add up to a pattern of strange occurrences that cannot be intelligently dismissed—or forgotten. Learn the truth about these mysterious sightings and who's attempting to cover them up.

0-7387-0106-8

264 pp., 6 x 9 $12.95

Time Travel
A New Perspective

J. H. BRENNAN

Scattered throughout the world are the skeletal remains of men and women from long before humanity appeared on the planet, and a human footprint contemporary with the dinosaurs. Where did they come from? Are these anomalies the litter left by time travelers from our own distant future? *Time Travel* is an extraordinary trip through some of the most fascinating discoveries of archaeology and physics, indicating that not only is time travel theoretically possible, but that future generations may actually be engaged in it. In fact, the latest findings of physicists show that time travel, at a subatomic level, is already taking place. Unique to this book is the program—based on esoteric techniques and the findings of parapsychology and quantum physics—which enables you to structure your own group investigation into a form of vivid mental time travel.

1-56718-085-X
224 pp., 6 x 9, photos $12.95

How to Be a Ghost Hunter
RICHARD SOUTHALL

So you want to investigate a haunting? This book is full of practical advice used in the author's own ghost-hunting practice. Find out whether you're dealing with a ghost, spirit, or an entity . . . and discover the one time when you should stop what you're doing and call in an exorcist. Learn the four-phase procedure for conducting an effective investigation, how to capture paranormal phenomena on film, record disembodied sounds and voices on tape, assemble an affordable ghost-hunting kit, and form your own paranormal group.

For anyone with time and little money to spend on equipment, this book will help you maintain a healthy sense of skepticism and thoroughness while you search for authentic evidence of the paranormal.

0-7387-0312-5
216 pp., 5³⁄₁₆ x 8, photos $12.95

Spanish edition:
Espíritus y fantasmas
0-7387-0382-6 $12.95

Monsters
An Investigator's Guide to Magical Beings

JOHN MICHAEL GREER

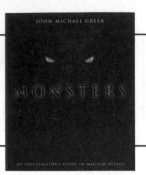

Most of us don't believe that entities such as vampires, shape-shifters, and faeries really exist. Even those who study UFOs or psychic powers dismiss them as unreal.

The problem is, people still keep running into them.

What do you do when the world you think you inhabit tears open, and something terrifying comes through the gap? Join ceremonial magician John Michael Greer as he takes you on a harrowing journey into the reality of the impossible. In *Monsters* he examines the most common types of beings still encountered in the modern world—vampires, ghosts, werewolves (and other shapeshifters), faeries, mermaids, dragons, spirits, angels, and demons—surveying what is known about them and how you can deal with their antics.

0-7387-0050-9
320 pp., 7½ x 9⅛, illus. $19.95

Grave's End
A True Ghost Story

ELAINE MERCADO

When Elaine Mercado and her first husband bought their home in Brooklyn, N.Y., in 1982, they had no idea that they and their two young daughters were embarking on a 13-year nightmare.

This book is the true story of how one family tried to adjust to living in a haunted house. It also tells how, with the help of parapsychologist Dr. Hans Holzer and medium Marisa Anderson, they discovered the identity of the ghosts and were able to assist them to the "light."

0-7387-0003-7
192 pp., 6 x 9 $12.95

Spanish edition:
Apariciones
0-7387-0214-5 $12.95

To order, call 1-877-NEW-WRLD
Prices subject to change without notice

To Write to the Authors

If you wish to contact the authors or would like more information about this book, please write to the authors in care of Llewellyn Worldwide and we will forward your request. Both the authors and publisher appreciate hearing from you and learning of your enjoyment of this book and how it has helped you. Llewellyn Worldwide cannot guarantee that every letter written to the authors can be answered, but all will be forwarded. Please write to:

Rob MacGregor and Bruce Gernon
℅ Llewellyn Worldwide
2143 Wooddale Drive, Dept. 0-7387-0757-0
Woodbury, MN 55125-2989, U.S.A.

Please enclose a self-addressed stamped envelope for reply,
or $1.00 to cover costs. If outside U.S.A., enclose
international postal reply coupon.

Many of Llewellyn's authors have websites with additional information and resources. For more information, please visit our website at:

www.llewellyn.com